SEEDS FOR LIFE

The Lifeseeds Core Curriculum for Living in Full Expression

A Whole New Way of Seeing Yourself

A Whole New Way of Being Yourself

A Whole New Way of Freeing Yourself

DAWN RICHERSON

© 2015, Dawn Richerson
All Rights Reserved

SEEDS FOR LIFE:
The Lifeseeds Core Curriculum for Living In Full Expression

Published by Lifeseeds Press
Atlanta, GA

ISBN 978-0-9887947-1-9 Print
ISBN 978-1-942969-99-0 E-book

This book may not be reproduced in whole or in part, without written permission from the author, except by a reviewer who may quote brief passages. Nor may any part of this book be reproduced, stored in a retrieval system, or transmitted in any form or by any means electronic, mechanical, photocopying, recording, scanning or otherwise.

Please note that all materials shared in this course are protected by U.S. copyright. You may use them for your personal use only. The materials may only be shared in a group or with other individuals when you purchase a license to use them. Please learn more or contact me through my website.

You may wish to explore *Seeds for Life* and the Lifeseeds Core Curriculum through the 90 Days to Life Online Experience. This experience provides lifetime access to videos for all core passages and daily seeds for life and the complete Lifeseeds video and audio collections. You may join the online experience at 90DaystoLife.com or from the Soul Store on the author's website at DawnRicherson.com.

Library of Congress Control Number: 2015905731
Printed in the United States of America

AUTHOR WEBSITE
www.DawnRicherson.com

For all who dare to enter in
to the unshakable kingdom and know
the threefold flame they are.

I Am Light • I Am Life • I Am Love

CONTENTS

Welcome and Introduction

A New Vision for Life Education

About the Lifeseeds Approach

Getting Started

A Whole New Way of Seeing Yourself

Introduction to the Life Formation Journey

Lifeseed #1—**Begin with Light**

Lifeseed #2—**Seek Illumination Within**

Lifeseed #3—**Make Room for a New Story**

Lifeseed #4—**Embrace Wholeness**

Lifeseed #5—**Connect to Your Still Center**

Lifeseed #6—**Hear the Song Rising Up, Remember**

Lifeseed #7—**Be a Part of the Universal Symphony**

Lifeseed #8—**Trust Yourself to Know the Tune**

Lifeseed #9—**Welcome All into the Guest House**

Lifeseed #10—**Tune to the Vibration of the Holy "Yes!"**

Lifeseed #11—**Be the River, See with New Eyes**

Lifeseed #12—**Choose to Honor Choice**

Lifeseed #13—**Be Here. Be Now. Be Now Here.**

Lifeseed #14—**Surprise! Get a Sense of Humor**

Lifeseed #15—**Live the Magic, Dance with Mystery**

Lifeseed #16—**Know You Are Loved, Beyond Measure**

Lifeseed #17—**See Life as Multidimensional Reality**

Lifeseed #18—**Open to Infinite Possibility**

Lifeseed #19—**Be Found in the Great I Am**

Lifeseed #20—**Surrender to Love**

Lifeseed #21—**Observe Life Working in Your Favor**

Lifeseed #22—**Unbind Yourself, Come to the Present**

Lifeseed #23—**Know You Are Well**

Lifeseed #24—**No Mistake Can Be Your Grave**

Lifeseed #25—**See You Are Inseparable from Love**

Lifeseed #26—**Weave a Home of Beauty**

Lifeseed #27—**Feel the Tender Mercies of Becoming**

Lifeseed #28—**Stand Amazed at Life Unfolding**

Lifeseed #29—**Dare to Take a Single Step**

Lifeseed #30—**Belong to All That Is**

Lifeseed #31—**Allow Yourself to Be Broken Open**

Lifeseed #32—**Let Love Be the Fuel**

Lifeseed #33—**Breathe In and Be on the Way**

Lifeseed #34—**Dare to Believe in Life**

Lifeseed #35—**Choose This Day**

Lifeseed #36—**Listen for Life's True Tones**

Lifeseed #37—**Know You Are Safe in Space and Time**

Lifeseed #38—**Be Free-Spirited in This Life, for Giving**

Lifeseed #39—**Share Fine Gifts of Original Design**

A Whole New Way of Being Yourself

Introduction to the Life Reformation Journey

Lifeseed #40—**Remember the Dream We Dreamed**

Lifeseed #41—**Hear All that Will Come to You in Silence**

Lifeseed #42—**Raise Your Voice to Find Your Truth**

Lifeseed #43—**Stay Current**

Lifeseed #44—**Allow Your Heart to Experience Change**

Lifeseed #45—**Know You Have All You Need**

Lifeseed #46—**Breathe Deeply and Welcome Life's Flow**

Lifeseed #47—**Hold Sacred the Freedom that Is Your Birthright**

Lifeseed #48—**See the Holy in the Ordinary**

Lifeseed #49—**Choose Your Mirror, Set the Scene**

Lifeseed #50—**Flex the Muscle of Your Mind**

Lifeseed #51—**Return to Love**

Lifeseed #52—**Open to Full Awareness as You Love What Is**

Lifeseed #53—**Ease into Life's Curves**

Lifeseed #54—**Stay Awake for the Journey**

Lifeseed #55—**Find a Way around Blocks**

Lifeseed #56—**Begin with Gratitude and Compassion**

Lifeseed #57—**Give Thanks for All that Nourishes**

Lifeseed #58—**Get in the Story**

Lifeseed #59—**Find Favor, Not Fault**

Lifeseed #60—**Cultivate Cooperation**

Lifeseed #61—**See Truth When It Surprises You**

Lifeseed #62—**Treasure the Dance of Life**

Lifeseed #63—**Let Go of a Need for Compensation**

Lifeseed #64—**Listen to Your Body**

Lifeseed #65—**Know Where You Belong**

Lifeseed #66—**Love Yourself First**

Lifeseed #67—**Notice How You Are Moving through Life**

Lifeseed #68—**Balance Work, Play, and Rest**

Lifeseed #69—**Stand in the Stream of Your Life**

Lifeseed #70—**Carry Your Truth in Grace**

Lifeseed #71—**Listen for the Song of Your Soul**

A Whole New Way of Freeing Yourself

Introduction to the Life Transformation Journey

Lifeseed #72—**Move to the Music of the Questions**

Lifeseed #73—**See Yourself as a Cycle of Change**

Lifeseed #74—**Engage in Value Redefinition**

Lifeseed #75—**Stand in Sacred Time**

Lifeseed #76—**Breathe in Promise Revealed**

Lifeseed #77—**See the Intricate Beauty of Life Unfolding**

Lifeseed #78—**Know that Beauty Begins Within**

Lifeseed #79—**Find What Feels Good**

Lifeseed #80—**Choose and Choose Again**

Lifeseed #81—**Find the Experience that Brings Out Your Best**

Lifeseed #82—**Cultivate Perspective and Balance**

Lifeseed #83—**Consider Form and Function**

Lifeseed #84—**Embrace Change**

Lifeseed #85—**Celebrate Choice and Creative Contribution**

Lifeseed #86—**Hold Fast to the Truth of Who You Are**

Lifeseed #87—**Unbind Yourself and Fly Free**

Lifeseed #88—**Risk the Journey**

Lifeseed #89—**Retain Your Sense of Play and Adventure**

Lifeseed #90—**Know the End Is the Beginning Again**

Your Journey from Here

Sharing Lifeseeds

"Life is a journey of discovering who it is we really are and who we have come to be. Life invites us to awaken the world within for a new beginning, find our forward flow, and embrace a new vision for the nexus of change. I believe with my whole heart this is a journey that can set us free to be who we came here to be."

DAWN RICHERSON

Welcome and Introduction

"We all want to live **a happy life** and have a right to do so,
whether through work or spiritual practice. I'm subject to destructive emotions
like anger and jealousy the same as you, but we all have **potential for good**.
However, our existing education system is oriented towards material development,
neglecting **inner values**. Consequently we lack a clear awareness
of the inner values that are the basis of a happy life."

~ Dalai Lama

WE ALL DESIRE HAPPINESS. We have come here, essentially, to experience life and the life more abundant. We are here now to experience the full glory and magnificence of who we are. Placed before us in this life is the unique opportunity to contribute to the full expression of humanity by simply being who we are. We are born into this world as powerful creators, agents of change fully designed and equipped to share fine gifts of original design. We have all we need to come fully to our lives and live in full expression; yet, we have forgotten what matters most.

We have forgotten that we are, as we are now, whole and complete. We have forgotten that we are a dynamic and sustainable system with access to inner resources that are the foundation for thriving and flourishing individually and in community. We have lost something vital. The full reclamation and radiant realization of who we are is our first and foremost responsibility, individually and collectively.

For too long, we have ignored the most essential subject of all: life. How does one successfully navigate its unpredictable twists and turns? How do we awaken the revelation of the mystery within and begin anew? How do we find a state of flow with so many obstacles and blocks to what our souls most desire? How can we become the revolution of love that, when we allow ourselves to see rightly and fully, we know we have come to be?

These are the questions that matter most. In all our pursuits for knowledge and mastery, we left them behind. We lost our way. Life is a journey of discovering who it is we really are and who we have come to be. Life invites us to awaken the world within for a new beginning, find our forward flow, and embrace a new vision for the nexus of change. I believe with my whole heart this is a journey that can set us free to be who we came here to be.

As more and more of us explore the territory of our souls, we will come to live in a radiantly expanded world where there is more life for all. We will recognize our own potential for good and share our gifts, receiving in kind the unique offerings of those with whom we share this journey we call life. We will find our joy and know our truth. The world will open up, changed, because we will be changed.

At its heart, the Lifeseeds core curriculum and the "90 Days to Life" online experience extend an invitation to the dance of your life and to the unfolding dance of humanity. It is a new day and the dawning of our lives, individually and collectively. There is no greater calling than the call of the soul. Listen to your life. Listen for the song rising up within you. Say "yes" to your life by coming fully to it and living in full expression.

I am delighted to be on the way with you, and it is my honor to share this work with you. It is my deepest desire that, together, we partake of life and enjoy a life more abundant. There is a vast and untapped treasure and a potential for good within each one of us. May we dare life's journey and follow the trail marked by these seeds for life, finding our way back to the light, life, and love that will lead us back into its current. I am excited to see where we go from here.

As you move into an exploration of these seeds for life, pause for a moment and consider the invitation to your life's dance. What experience of life do you most desire? What are you seeking? What is your soul longing to express? Hold in your heart a vision for your life, radiantly expanded, and open to new possibilities as you embark on life's grand and daring adventure.

With such love for humanity and with deep honor for your life's unfolding journey,

Dawn

Dawn Richerson
January 15, 2015

A New Vision for Life Education

I BELIEVE DEEPLY THAT NOW IS THE TIME for a radical reinvention in education that is oriented to inner values and a thriving life. An expansion of our definition of life education is in order. We can no longer afford the luxury of pretending that soul growth and spiritual evolution are somehow a separate matter from thriving in life. Nor can we create schools and educational institutions focused exclusively on knowledge without any attention at all to the soul-inspired and heart-centered approaches to life and life's work that research has shown are integral to human flourishing and thriving. Learning that supports a whole new experience of life, individually and collectively, can only happen from the inside out. We begin within.

Remembering that we are, at our core, light, life, and love, and coming fully to our lives is not simply an individual pursuit undertaken purely for individual well-being. It is also good stewardship. It is our contribution to the human story and to this good Earth that is our home. Without this foundation, we cannot fully share our unique gifts and offerings. Conversely, when we are fully immersed in the whole of who we are, connected to our whole self and our soul self, there is a natural flow that opens up in our lives. We find a whole new way of seeing ourselves, a whole new way of being ourselves, and a whole new way of freeing ourselves.

I am honored to share a birthdate with Dr. Martin Luther King, Jr. He had a dream for his four children. He had a dream for humanity. Spurred on by that dream, he planted the seeds of a great work with his life. Lifeseeds is born of my vision for a life more abundant, realized as we come to see ourselves as whole and complete, radiant and resplendent, created free and meant to live free. It was, in the beginning, a simple, heartfelt dream for myself, that I might discover those qualities of happiness, peace, and joy in my own life.

I have long been passionate about an inside-out approach to life and life's work. I began to notice that, when I started at my core with my soul's pureset desires and at the depths of my being, day by day, everything somehow fell into place. My life was expanded as I dared to connect to the three pathways of soul exploration, expression, and expansion. My dream for my own life has opened up into a realization that these seeds for life that have reconnected me with my essential self, journey, and truth, are meant to be shared.

I believe we are on the cusp of something wonderful, and it is my own experience that a reconnection to what is most essential, what matters most, is the key to a whole new you and a whole new world. It is time for a whole new way forward in our very approach to life. We need to see the damage done when we force a false separation between the life of the soul and the soul of our lives — that happiness and joy we long to experience more and more.

What's essential? What matters most? This question, or quest-Ion and I like to call it, leads us into an exploration of the inner life that is the only place to look for a firm foundation from which to expand into all we desire for our own lives and for the world.

This is my dream for a world radiantly expanded: I see a sea of soul-inspired people lit up by an array of their own colorful dreams for life shining forth as each individual connects to inner values and those fine gifts of original design and sacred seeds of essence he or she has come bearing. Only a view of ourselves and of the whole of humanity that begins with light, life, and love can lead us to the re-creation of our lives and our world. The Lifeseeds curriculum offers pathways or seeds for life to reconnect us with the light, life, and love that is foundational for a flourishing life.

My vision is that these simple seeds for life will bring new life to those individuals and groups who feel bound or trapped in systems, situations, and societies that seem designed to further restrict and squelch their free spirits. I would like to connect these concepts, which have opened me up to new possibility and so radically altered the course of my own life, with others who find themselves caught up in circumstances that have led them far afield from the inner light of truth. From hospital wards to prison cells, from youth detention centers to domestic violence programs, from homeless shelters to refugee camps, I have a vision of more and more of us set free from all that binds us or has us believing we are blocked from the light, life, and love we so desire.

The Lifeseeds core curriculum is truly the heart and soul of my work in the world and at the same time it is a gift for the whole of humanity. I am open to new ideas for ways to share it. If you are connected to a group or organization you feel could benefit from the seeds for life in this core curriculum, please reach out to discuss sharing the materials through a pilot program or as a licensed facilitator. If you would like to use Lifeseeds in your coaching or consulting practice, please send me an e-mail about your interest in becoming a licensed facilitator and I will contact you when the next opportunity is available.

About the Lifeseeds Approach

THE LIFESEEDS CORE CURRICULUM for living in full expression offers a deeper exploration of your essential self, your essential journey, and your essential truth. At the heart of the curriculum are ninety pathways that awaken us to greater purpose and meaning in our lives. I have likened these seeds for life to the starter for the sourdough bread I used to make. They are most useful when absorbed over time and allowed to rise from within.

These seeds activate the light within each individual and allow that individual's unique expression of the one light to shine through more clearly. They connect us to the life we are, and return us to our natural state of love. The process happens over time, almost without our noticing the profound changes taking place. It is the core practice of cultivating from our core the light, life, and love we are that leads us to full flourishing and the ability to water the world with the fullest expression of who we are.

The Lifeseeds curriculum and the "90 Days to Life" online experience are not intended to to produce adherence to yet another version of truth. Rather, Lifeseeds is catalyst for soul growth an expansion, the abundant and joy-filled experience of life, and our collective flourishing. As I have shared this core content in workshops, in groups, and with other individuals during the past three years, I have been struck by the varied ways a given seed for life awakens and activates those who encounter it. Each seed for life enhances the natural desire for life and supports the fullest expression of each individual's unique soul signature.

Our shared objective as we connect to these pathways is life itself. LIFE is an acronym for Living In Full Expression. We have come here for life. We have come to experience life and to welcome and share a life more abundant. The fulfillment of that objective results in happier lives. As more and more of us come fully to the life that is here and now, we create a whole new experience of our collective journey.

Essentially, these ninety seeds for life provide a map to connect you back to what that matters most. While on the surface simple and streamlined, this map is layered with levels of meaning and provides continued activation at a soul level and the revelation of treasures planted there. It is multidimensional, rather than linear. As you explore these seeds, connecting one at a time, you are watering the sacred seeds of essence alive and well within you. You are preparing the way so that your "fine gifts of original design" can be shared with the world. You are stepping into a whole new you and a whole new way forward through a whole new way of seeing yourself, being yourself, and freeing yourself.

The Lifeseeds core curriculum supports a life lived in full expression. The daily lifeseeds combine with your unique streams of soul to support you as you gather momentum in your life, leading you back into the current of now — this present moment that is, in fact, your next opportunity window. The key to the future is here and now, and it has been waiting within.

By engaging with these seeds for life, we enter into the formation, reformation, and transformation of our lives. These three processes are simultaneously unfolding within us as we embrace more of who we are. We are being formed, reformed, and transformed in holistic fashion. These three soul journeys are interwoven and embedded within the Lifeseeds core curriculum lead us back to life through this threefold process:

- **CORE CONNECTION**: We awaken the world within and embrace *a whole new way of seeing ourselves*, which allows us to remember who we are, reconnect to our essential self, and come fully to life. We begin with light and find our way from the inside out. This is the the process of life formation. We explore the territory of our souls along the path of soul exploration.

- **INTEGRATED FLOW:** We find our forward flow and embrace *a whole new way of being ourselves*, which allows us to connect threads of experience and the streams of our souls, reconnect to our essential journey, and experience a life more abundant. We see rivers of miracles spring forth from a single choice to believe in goodness, and we reframe the story of our lives, individually and collectively. We begin to express the streams of our soul along the path of soul expression.

- **RADIANT EXPANSION**: We embrace a new vision for our lives and *a whole new way of freeing ourselves*, which allows us to water the world with the fullest expression of who we are, reconnect to our essential truth, and walk in the way of life, experiencing ourselves *as* life. We move to the music of the questions and are revealed as mystery, even as we expand radiantly in our own singularly magnificent revolution of love. Along the path of soul expansion, we align our choices with the call of the soul and expand radiantly from within.

Getting Started

COMING FULLY TO YOUR LIFE AND EXPANDING RADIANTLY into the fullest expression of who you are: this is what life is all about. The seeds for life or "lifeseeds" included in the Lifeseeds curriculum provide pathways to greater purpose and meaning through the three interwoven movements of life formation, life reformation, and life transformation. These three movements are all unfolding at once within us, whether we are aware and connected or not.

This guide can be used in conjunction with the "90 Days to Life" online experience or on its own (use coupon code SEEDS20 for additional savings when you register at DawnRicherson.com/90-Days-to-Life-Experience. This guide can also supplement a workshop series led by a Lifeseeds facilitator or a group discussion setting within an organization. Whether you are working through the material solo at your own pace or as part of a larger experience, this format gives you easy access to these seeds for life, which offer ninety ways to cultivate YOU. Your daily encounter with these seeds for life engages the sacred seeds of essence within you, helping you to remember who you are as a soul so that you can water the world with the fullest expression of who you are.

Four Pillars of Soul Expansion

WHOLENESS. ABUNDANCE. EXPANSION. FLOW. These are the four pillars of the Lifeseeds core curriculum. They rise up from a seed that grows from within each human soul and its unique reflection of the One light that is our shared Source, that common bond of humanity. That shared Source from which endless pools of soul flow forth contains the indestructible qualities of wholeness, abundance, expansion, and flow. It is life-seeking, life-affirming, and life-enhancing.

This is the unapologetic foundation of Lifeseeds, which is neither an exclusively religious nor a strictly secular offering. This core curriculum honors your chosen spiritual path, whatever that may be, and it invites you into a soulful experience of yourself. It is intrinsically life-centered, with every seed reconnecting you to the life within. These seeds for life are for individual thriving, and they are for a flourishing humanity. The four pillars create a temple of experience into which you may enter. Yet, your experience will be unique, for it is your essential self, journey, and truth that is revealed as you pass through the portal opened by each of the seeds for life.

Three Truths, Three Journeys

THE THREEFOLD JOURNEY OF LIFESEEDS is the journey of a soul. This experience naturally supports radiant expansion in your life and in your life's work by immersing you in the streams of your soul. The interwoven processes of formation, reformation, and transformation are three streams that help us remember who we are as we connect to our core and awaken the world within, find our forward flow, and embrace a new vision for our lives.

My own journey has led me into an experience of three essential truths: 1) I am light, 2) I am life, 3) I am love. When fully integrated, these truths open up a path to a fuller experience and expression of your life. These are the three truths revealed through our exploration of the seeds for life in the Lifeseeds core curriculum. We begin within, at the still center point of our souls, and affirm that we are light, life, and love. Let's consider each of these briefly.

I AM LIGHT • When you connect to your core or to your essential self, you discover who you really are. A *whole new way of seeing* becomes possible. Your view of yourself and the world shifts dramatically, because the vantage point of the still center, where true power resides, provides the fullest perspective, a full-circle view of life from the point of choice that is your point of power. During the Life Formation Journey, we walk the path of soul exploration and awaken the world within. We remember we are light.

I AM LIFE • When you connect to the flow of your life, integrating the whole of your life's unique experience and your essential journey with the larger perspective of who you are as a soul, *a whole new way of being* is possible. You begin to express who you are with confidence and grace. During the Life Reformation Journey, we will walk the path of soul expression and find our forward flow. We remember we are life and allow all experience to flow from that stream of life that is eternal and self-renewing.

I AM LOVE • When you connect to your soul's deepest truths and desires and to your essential truth, you find a *whole new way of freeing* yourself. You are expanded radiantly and connect to dreams and a newfound joy for your life and your life's work. You begin to see that you are not meant to shrink into a role or designated function; you are meant to soar, to spark your own unique revolution of love in the world. During the Life Transformation Journey, we will walk the path of soul expansion. We remember we are love.

Guidelines for Daily Practice

WHILE THE SIMPLE TRUTHS CONTAINED within this life curriculum may at times seem obvious, there are many layers to each of the momentum action pathways opened up by each seed for life. As you are moving through the material for the first time, whether through this guide or as part of the "90 Days to Life" experience, I recommend fifteen minutes to digest everything that is provided each day and an additional fifteen minutes for reflection and an exploration of the Daily DARE {Daring Adventure in Radiant Expansion} and meditation.

As you move through this course, I invite you to approach with an open heart and adopt the following guidelines:

- **Come fully to this practice.** Come without distraction. If possible create a consistent routine as you consider what is here for you.

- **Release expectation and open to possibility.** You are not working to earn something. You are dancing with your soul, getting to know it by becoming the observer of your life's unfolding, and listening for the song of yourself. You are showing up fully as you for you.

- **Clear a space.** Clear your mind. Before you begin each day, clear your field by stepping outside if possible or connecting to your physical body.

- **Ask for discernment and guidance.** Ask to be led to what your soul desires to show you. Take a moment to set an intention before you begin this course and do so again each new day. Ask and you shall receive.

- **Keep a Lifeseeds Journal.** Include questions, dialogue journaling with your soul self, and new awareness about your essential self, journey, and truth.

- **Smile, laugh, love, live.** Look for joy. Seek the gifts hidden in plain sight. Know you are loved beyond measure, and look for the evidence of this truth.

Daily Points of Connection

EACH DAY'S LESSON WILL INCLUDE:

- An **Opening Context** that sets the stage for the collective journey of humanity and common touch points on the individual journey of a soul through this life. This first paragraph is excerpted from one of the three acts in the narrated "Story of Life." This journey is available at DawnRicherson.com/story-of-life.

- A **Focus Text** or core passage from the *Cultivating Essence* book series with the option to read the text, listen to an audio, or watch a video.

- A **Daily Lifeseed**, which offers further reflection on and an expansion of the core passage.

- **A Daily DARE** (Daring Adventure in Radiant Expansion) to grow your soul and expand radiantly through a deeper exploration of the daily pathway.

{1}
Life Formation
for Core Connection

Awaken the World Within
A Whole New Way of Seeing Yourself

Introduction to the Life Formation Journey

The Life Formation Journey focuses on core connection to awaken the world within. We begin with a reconnection to your essential self. Together, let's connect to the Path of Soul Exploration. This journey introduces you to a whole new way of seeing yourself. Think of the pathways or seeds for life below as invitations to further explore the territory of your soul and awaken the world within for a new beginning. In this first journey, we are remembering, **I AM LIGHT**.

About Life Formation Lifeseeds

Think of the momentum action pathways (MAPs) below as living maps that support you as you further explore the territory of your soul and awaken the world within for a new beginning. These seeds for life and the pathways they open up correspond to passages found in the first movement of *Cultivating Essence from the Matrix of Soul* and are further explored in the book, *Awakening the World Within*, available from my website.

Seeds for Life from the Life Formation Soul Journey

LIFE FORMATION LIFESEEDS

1. BEGIN WITH LIGHT
2. SEEK ILLUMINATION FROM WITHIN
3. MAKE ROOM FOR A NEW STORY
4. EMBRACE WHOLENESS
5. CONNECT TO YOUR STILL CENTER
6. HEAR THE SONG RISING UP, REMEMBER
7. BE A PART OF THE UNIVERSAL SYMPHONY
8. TRUST YOURSELF TO KNOW THE TUNE
9. WELCOME ALL INTO THE GUEST HOUSE
10. TUNE TO THE VIBRATION OF THE HOLY "YES!"
11. BE THE RIVER, SEE WITH NEW EYES
12. CHOOSE TO HONOR CHOICE
13. BE HERE. BE NOW. BE NOW HERE.
14. SURPRISE! GET A SENSE OF HUMOR
15. LIVE THE MAGIC, DANCE WITH MYSTERY
16. KNOW YOU ARE LOVED, BEYOND MEASURE
17. SEE LIFE AS MULTIDIMENSIONAL REALITY
18. OPEN TO INFINITE POSSIBILITY
19. BE FOUND IN THE GREAT I AM
20. SURRENDER TO LOVE
21. OBSERVE LIFE WORKING IN YOUR FAVOR
22. UNBIND YOURSELF, COME TO THE PRESENT
23. KNOW YOU ARE WELL

24. NO MISTAKE CAN BE YOUR GRAVE
25. SEE YOU ARE INSEPARABLE FROM LOVE
26. WEAVE A HOME OF BEAUTY
27. FEEL THE TENDER MERCIES OF BECOMING
28. STAND AMAZED AT LIFE UNFOLDING
29. DARE TO TAKE A SINGLE STEP
30. BELONG TO ALL THAT IS
31. ALLOW YOURSELF TO BE BROKEN OPEN
32. LET LOVE BE THE FUEL
33. BREATHE IN & BE ON THE WAY
34. DARE TO BELIEVE IN LIFE
35. CHOOSE THIS DAY
36. LISTEN FOR LIFE'S TRUE TONES
37. KNOW YOU ARE SAFE IN SPACE & TIME
38. BE FREE-SPIRITED IN THIS LIFE, FOR GIVING
39. SHARE FINE GIFTS OF ORIGINAL DESIGN

Lifeseed #1—Begin with Light

1

We begin with light. Once upon a time, Light.
In the beginning, light: One light, radiant and resplendent.

FOCUS TEXT
The Story of Beginnings

Each of the world's monotheistic religious traditions shares the concept of light. In the beginning: light. Light born of darkness. Light called forth. Light being lit. Light bursting forth. Light drawing us toward it. Light within us. Light not fully understood.

In the beginning God created the heavens and the earth. Now the earth was formless and empty, darkness was over the surface of the deep, and the Spirit of God was hovering over the waters. And God said, "Let there be light," and there was light. God saw that the light was good, and he separated the light from darkness.
  ~ from the Judeo-Christian tradition, Genesis 1:1-2, The Torah

Allah is the Light of the heavens and the earth. The Parable of His Light is as if there were a Niche and within it a Lamp: the Lamp enclosed in Glass: the glass as it were a brilliant star: Lit from a blessed Tree, an Olive, neither of the east nor of the west, whose oil is well-nigh luminous, though fire scarce touched it: Light upon Light! Allah doth guide whom He will to His Light: Allah doth set forth Parables for men: and Allah doth know all things.
  ~ from the Islamic tradition, Surah 24. An-Nur (Light), 35, The Koran, (Yusuf Ali Translation)

In the beginning was the Word, and the Word was with God, and the Word was God. He was with God in the beginning. Through him all things were made, without him nothing was made that had been made. In him was life, and that life was the light of men. The light shines in the darkness, but the darkness has not understood it.
~ from the Christian tradition, John 1:1-5, The Bible (New International Version)

LIFESEED
Begin with Light

In the beginning, Light. I am and you are light, born of the One Light, radiant and resplendent. The root of our life's energy is light. The world's great teachers and religions have pointed us in this direction throughout time, yet we so often have separated ourselves from the light that is the essence of all life. We must tend to that inner light, returning to its deep well. There in our souls resides an inexhaustible supply of all we have been seeking.

You may doubt that light is there. Seek it, and you will find it. Embrace a whole new way of seeing yourself and your life as you look for light rather that seeking evidence of your lack of light. Light is the very foundation of life. We have simply become invisible to its life within us.

The Light you seek is seeking you. It will always be there for us, waiting for our full reunion with it at the tree of life. You will find that tree in the garden of your soul, that place of creation and re-creation within where all things are restored to their true nature. There, in the center of your life, you will find your resting place and your place of beginning again. Begin with light and seek daily to return to that light you are.

DAILY DARE
Look for Light Today

Today, look for the light in all you observe. Keep a notebook or recording device with you through the day and record the light you see reflected in all that is set before you. Then set aside time to consider each more carefully, giving thanks for all the ways the light is reflected back to you. In your Lifeseeds Journal, express your gratitude and appreciation for the light within you that has made it possible for you to recognize such beauty and the play of light in the world around you. Today's dare corresponds to the "Looking for the Light" tool from the Lifeseeds Toolkit.

Lifeseed #2—Seek Illumination Within

2

Such sweeping magnificence was ours. We came close to touching glory. But despite the cultural and technological wonders we created, we lost our way and fell in time into a deep slumber. Roaming around in a self-created darkness, we forgot we were eternal lights, carriers of sacred seeds of essence that held the promise of a new world.

FOCUS TEXT
Eternal Lights

Our world has never needed light more. Our lives have never needed light more. Yet, the busy pace of our lives and the rapid evolution of new technologies in our time have, for all their improvements, only exposed the fact that what is merely external can never illuminate that which lies inside the human heart.

While the continued unfolding of new technology and the exploration of new frontiers is important work, we stand now on the precipice of an awakening that begins within. Now it is time to explore the interior truths that can only emerge when we, individually and collectively, embrace the light shining beyond that darkness we have perceived to be held within that vast unknown and unexplored territory of our hearts.

We have been afraid to go too deep, afraid of what might lurk within the recesses of our hearts and minds. We know too well the wounds of this world. Even those of us who have embraced healing and invested significant resources in cleaning up thoughts, emotions and behaviors have held onto an outdated belief that this is work — and hard work at that.

Some of us have become experts at roaming around in the darkness we perceive within. Courageously, a few among us have dared to open the vast unknown within to a source of light we have perceived to be outside ourselves, perhaps from some far-off deity or from the enlightenment of more evolved souls who have journeyed through this world. We have been reaching for a solution that comes from outside ourselves.

The truth is that we have all the light we need. We carry it within. Nothing external is needed. What *is* needed is an awakening to the worlds within. In this time of great change, humanity faces a choice. Will we awaken to the truth that we are eternal lights shining in darkness? Or will we continue to scramble in some last-ditch effort to fix the darkness we see as closing in upon us? Will we choose illumination or will we remain entrenched in the illusion of separation?

LIFESEED
Seek Illumination Within

Many of us carry that early memory of being afraid of the dark. The unknown seemed vast. Perhaps we were afraid we would be swallowed up or lost within that darkness. Somehow, through the years, we began to focus more on the absence of light in our lives and became blind to the source of light we carry within.

We have long chased the light, convincing ourselves that if only we run far enough and fast enough, we will catch a glimmer of shining radiance and all will be well. Like a pack of hungry, howling wolves, we have covered many miles beneath the moonlight. We sleep. We hurt. We eat. We are always searching, looking for the way forward.

Somewhere in the dream of our lives, if we awaken to what is, we find a mysterious light in our forested heart and follow its strange glow to the edge of all we have known. We are astonished by the recollection of all we have been seeking contained within the vessels we are. Protected there, by the blessed tree of life within us, is an everlasting light, and it is the seed of who you are — eternally light, indivisible and whole. When you embrace a whole new way of seeing yourself by beginning with light and seeking that light within, everything changes. Your world opens up.

DAILY DARE
You Are the Lighthouse

Today, just for this one day, seek no external advice, counsel, or guidance. Trust fully that you have all the light you need. See yourself as the lighthouse, and seek illumination about the next right step in your life from within. Write about this experience in your Lifeseeds Journal. Today's dare corresponds to the "Trusting Your Inner Light" tool from the Lifeseeds Toolkit.

Lifeseed #3—Make Room for a New Story

3

The accomplishments of humanity were world-changing, life-changing. Still, it unraveled. Even in our undoing life was beautiful. Even so, through the ages, we began to feel alone. So alone. Helpless. Unable to fix the broken things, to make peace among the warring factions, to feed the hungry child. We sat, huddled in darkness, buckled beneath the weight of it all. We began to see the light as separate from us and ourselves as undeserving of its warmth.

We were lost in a story of separation.

FOCUS TEXT
Separating Light from Darkness

Before any of us can hope to bring forth the light within, or even to see through the darkness to which we have grown accustomed, we must release the old beliefs about ourselves to which we cling in desperation. We have long believed ourselves to be a people immersed in the shadow of this world, wanderers through a cold, dark night or vagabonds blinded by the desert's stinging sun and sand.

Make room for a new story, the creation of a wondrous wave upon whose crest rides the hope of humanity. Even now, the beating of a million hearts echo with a longing to rush toward the shores of a new understanding of who we are as beings of light. We long to know our light, thanks in large part to those pioneering souls among us who have called us, again and again, back to this truth.

Awakening to the light within begins by acknowledging the darkness we have known so well and then separating out that darkness or our perception of it to allow light to emerge. What darkness have we known? Separation within. Separation without. Division within. Division without. Chaos within. Chaos without. Addiction. Brokenness. Disease. War. Alienation. Poverty. Inequality. Subjugation. Devastation and deconstruction. Waste. What am I forgetting?

Having identified and called out the darkness we know, it is time to see what does not belong to the darkness and to give it equal consideration. Faith, flowing where there seems to be no evidence or cause. Hope, springing up in the most unlikely of circumstance. Love, mirrored in the eyes of those we encounter every day.

Once we begin to see the light all around us, breaking forth through any darkness, we are able to trace it back to the seed from which it grew. How did this light find its way out into our world? What is the source of the faith, hope and love we encounter? And how is this light, born of ordinary people from all walks of life, a reflection of the one light within you?

Where in you can you separate out light and call it good?

LIFESEED

Make Room for a New Story

To make way for a new life we are called to create a spaciousness. As we listen to our "Once Upon a Time," we will be led back to the middle — that still center point from which All That Is emanates. This is the inception of the story of life from which we have been creating. How does the story you have been telling about who you are and how your life is unfolding feel from this place? Is it the whole of the story?

In the end, it is always about beginning again. We may return to the center of our lives and trust life to reveal an opening. Open yourself to the possibility that you are more than who you think you are, that life is an ever-expanding sphere of possibility in which you may become. In stillness, allow for the formation of something you have not yet begun to imagine.

Begin to look for all you have been missing by beginning with the light within. In the end, everything leads back to light, and as we are beginning to step into that light it is sometimes useful to see it around us and realize that to see and know this outward reflection of light indicates it is present within us. Allow the stillness to shed a little light on the truth of who you are underneath all the stories you have accepted about who you are, then step into a whole new way of seeing who you are.

DAILY DARE
Enter into Stillness

Today, make room for a new story with a full five minutes of every waking hour of complete stillness: body, mind, heart, and soul. In the days that follow set aside at least five full minutes for complete stillness. Write about your soulful experience of quiet and stillness in your Lifeseeds Journal. Today's dare corresponds to the "You Are the Lighthouse" tool from the Lifeseeds Toolkit.

Lifeseed #4—Embrace Wholeness

4

Shivering, we numbed ourselves to the lie we told: "There is no light here for me. I am nothing. We are sinners, undeserving of love and the life more abundant." Succumbing to this illusion, we created a reality based on false foundations. Through all the ages, more and more of us passed through this life in a sort of perpetual spin cycle. We forgot our choice to choose. We forgot who we are: whole wonders of creation, creators of a whole new world. Caught up in illusion, we built a world and forgot we were enough, whole, complete. At last we awaken, gathering up silvery threads and golden strands, weaving the world within and without. We begin anew, drawing on the light within.

FOCUS TEXT
The Life Within Lights Our Way

In every moment there is a point of choice. Will we move upward and expand outward along the ever-widening spiral of our lives? Or will we contract and, slipping down, revert to a sort of sleeping sickness? Or, perhaps more damning, will we succumb to the illusion that there is no choice at all and simply pass through this life and this world in a sort of perpetual spin cycle?

We choose the meaning we attach to the events of our lives and that choice sets us in motion in one direction or another. It is never about what happens. It is always about what we tell ourselves about what happens. More accurately, it is about the story we tell ourselves about who we must be because some certain thing has happened. It only means what meaning we choose to assign. This is a difficult truth to grasp.

We have passed the time of excuses. You alone sculpt your reality. You alone shape the future you will experience. You are now responsible for everything that happens in your inner environment. What happens around you is simply a reflection of what alone or through collusion you have allowed to be planted in the sacred garden of your hearts and souls. If you want a good gauge of how you are doing, take a look around.

But this is not to say that all is lost. You may go back now and reshape your reality by choosing a new interpretation, by seeing that what you have believed is merely one possible version of the truth. Experiment by choosing a meaning that also allows you to stand fully in your power as the creator of your life and also allows others to be in harmony with the whole of who they are and their expression of their true selves at any given point in time. Release the need for perfection and embrace wholeness. In so doing, you will uncover the unfathomable uniqueness of who you truly are.

LIFESEED
Embrace Wholeness

We look and see the pieces, scattered fragments and parts unassembled. Some of us look within and see a mess — disjointed shapes and forms in contrasting colors. Who knows what to do with this?

We have merely forgotten that we are the sovereign shapers of our lives, fully equipped to reshape ourselves by loving all we are. We may choose to see ourselves as whole by valuing the whole of who we are.

Are you creating *from within* all you dream for your life? Close your eyes and see the light that lives inside of you. From this place, you are free to see yourself as a system, dynamic and sustainable, completely equipped for the wondrous dance of your life here and now.

DAILY DARE

Stand Within the Expanding Sphere You Are

Today, each time you think of a lack or a deficiency, breathe in deeply and remember your wholeness. Pause for a moment and envision yourself in the center of a sphere that is naturally expanding to the degree that you allow. Envision all the resources and energy you need held within the field of this sphere. Give thanks for the wholeness of who you are. Write a statement in your Lifeseeds Journal to remind you of your wholeness and to express your gratitude for this awareness. Today's dare corresponds to the "Whole Systems Thinking" tool from the Lifeseeds Toolkit.

Lifeseed #5—Connect to Your Still Center

5

We found ourselves pricked by life, wounded to the core.
We hurt so much, some of us cursed the very nature of who we are.
We went less and less to that sacred space within. All the while,
we scrambled, feeling more and more disconnected… from each
other and from ourselves. We longed for reconnection to each other.
We have only just begun to understand this: the key
to interconnectivity is inner connectivity.

FOCUS TEXT

The Key to Interconnectivity Is Inner Connectivity

Begin at your core. See the beautiful lines that connect one facet of who you are to the other. Discover the seeds that are hidden in plain sight within your heart. We open up, fullness into fullness, from the tiniest seed of infinite possibility. And it is such a fragile process.

We hurt when that tiny seed is pricked by life.

Sometimes we hurt so much we curse the seed and deny the very essence of who we are. To do so is to ignore the very thing that might give us wings and set us free. We are meant to live from wholeness, to connect to that first and then to each other. Connect deeply and often to your still center. God is there. You are there.

LIFESEED

Connect to Your Still Center

On the surface of things, we see ourselves and think we know the whole. But dive deeper now and dare to see. Gaze into the looking glass and in the stillness find some lost ripple of truth. You are wonder, come to life, a beautiful diamond of a star, shining with reflected light that, mysteriously, emanates from some place where Spirit stirs in stillness.

Perhaps you are remembering now a time in the past when you looked and scary things rose from those inner waters — or you found some image there of a self you did not wish to see. You are safe. You are loved. All is well, and you can trust in life to hold you. The seed has not been squandered. You are not lost to self.

Deeply, gently, go within and see how all the threads are there. They are simply waiting to flow together again to form the texture of community. Look and look again. Connect to this dynamic core of your being and be free from all that would keep you separate and in pain.

DAILY DARE

Explore the World Within

Today, use crayons, colored pencils, or paint to create a representation of the beautiful lines that connect the unique variety and strands of self that resides within you. Use your imagination and allow your art to lead you where it wants to take you. Follow the flow. In your Lifeseeds Journal, record any insights you gather as you consider the whole of who you are. If you feel inspired to do so, express your gratitude for this new exploration of the world within you and the experience of being and becoming you would like to call forward in your life.

As you consider the light within, notice what comes into your awareness. Often, as we connect more deeply to the light we are, we naturally reconnect to the streams of our soul, including the sacred seeds of essence and fine gifts of original design we come bearing. Today's dare corresponds to the "Streams of Soul, Strands of Light" tool from the Lifeseeds Toolkit.

Lifeseed #6—Hear the Song Rising Up, Remember

6

So many of us caved beneath the pressure of others
defining us as someone small and splintered ourselves. We tuned
out the persistent alarms from within. Perhaps we retreated into the places
we felt safe. There were those who buried the seed of self beneath
an endless busyness or addiction. Over time, we silenced our song
and lost the tune. Still, somehow, our souls remembered.
As we awaken, we listen to our life's grace notes and
a magnificent melody born from within.

FOCUS TEXT
Waking Up

We are travelers on a common journey. The first step to the next step on that journey is for each of us, beginning in this moment, to clear limiting beliefs we have formed because others could not acknowledge the truth of their own souls and, as such, could not have dared to see us for who we truly are. The next step to the next step is to see our way back to our soul's inexpressible beauty and to celebrate that. Wildly!

There are easier ways to wake up than for your entire body to reverberate to the sound of a harsh doorbell at six o'clock in the morning. Yet, this is the situation you now find yourselves in. Listen for the gentle hum of your life. Almost imperceptible at first, it will stir you back into the opportunity of the moment.

In the stillness there is a song that rises up within you. And it is unlike the song of any other. It is yours alone to sing, and in the singing you will remember. As you remember more of who you have always been, your song will carry on the wind. And more of you will be awakened to your soul's song rising. And soon the universe will harmonize to the beauty of your voices, and your hearts will become an unstoppable chorus of change.

LIFESEED
Hear the Song Rising Up, Remember

Whose eyes have you been looking through? Is it any surprise you see what you see? Wake up and dream your own dream of your life. Find a place of solitude and begin with this: say aloud to yourself, "I celebrate me. I am free. I am free be. I am free to be fully me."

If you can't say it like you mean it, picture a wild fan of who you are, sitting in the stands celebrating your every move. You may or may not have met this fan, but go ahead. Climb inside your heart, take a look around, and do a happy dance as you discover you are being cheered on by a multitude of fans.

OK. Now, listen. Not to the noise and confusion likely swirling around you on any given day. Listen to the sound within the sound, the song you lost but knew by heart once upon a time. Be curious about the tune and the words that are your own.

You have a part in this life, and you are the star of your life. Without you, the world is incomplete. You are, as you are, whole and complete. Waiting within you, you have all you need.

DAILY DARE
A Musical Note

Today, write a musical "Light Note" to yourself to remind you of the beauty your life brings when you listen for the song that lives inside. Create a simple visual reminder, such as a quarter note or a drawing of you singing with your hand on your heart. Or create an original song or rap: "I used to hide from this world inside. Now I'm free to love the whole of me." Have fun! The idea is to create some reminder to listen for the song rising up from within. Write what you know of the song so far in your Lifeseeds Journal. Today's dare corresponds to the "Light Notes" tool from the Lifeseeds Toolkit.

Lifeseed #7—Be a Part of the Universal Symphony

7

Once upon a time, we were walking in a world...

Dancing in the dark, we lost the rhythm of our joy.

By the time we knew something was not as it was intended to be,

we could no longer find our way. We dismissed the laughter and

even the tears that might have led us back. Disconnected from

ourselves and from each other, we lost the music of our lives.

Reconciled one to another, the music rises. It is

the dawning of our lives.

FOCUS TEXT
Learning to Sing Again

You have learned in this life to curl up with your treasures, to cradle yourselves against those who might label you as "other than" and to safely tuck away the truth of who you are in an effort to guard yourself from attack. But your song is not meant only for you. The song of your soul is but one strain of a universal symphony. We must sing the world alive.

Some of you treasure your gift but only for yourselves. Others of you are frightened by the very sacred seed that lies within you, and so you bury it deeper and cover it with busy-ness, mindless activity, addiction and distraction. Over time, you fall into a deep sleep and the world is robbed of the richness of you. You are lost to your pseudo-selves, selves which fragment the one whole truth of who you are.

You must embrace the whole of who you are, but the embrace is not enough. You must share your soul self and watch the gift be multiplied. Find the fortitude and courage to step out onto the waves and know who you are is all you need. Sing out in faith and listen for the wind's reply.

Some of you convince yourselves that the faint song rising like a sun is only an imagining, wishful thinking or a futile longing for what can be no more. You are frightened by what wells up within you. You do not understand it. You do not want it.

Some of you want only to experience this physical realm in which your soul is housed and so set off on an arduous, careful journey to cover up what is within you. But the cost of doing so is steep. If you are to awaken the world, you must sing again the song of yourself.

LIFESEED
Be a Part of the Universal Symphony

Yesterday, perhaps, it seemed your life was easier. Maybe then you weren't so old or worn by life. Maybe then, you say, you could have learned to sing. You say it is too late. It doesn't matter anymore, anyway.

You matter. You do! The gift you are is a miracle, multiplied when shared. Will you dare to be still and present to the song you learned through time to silence? Sshhh. It's okay. It may take some time, and we've got all the time you need. What's more, you have everything it takes.

You may think finding goodness in your heart to be impossible. I say you can walk on water. Begin by taking this dare: today, be patient and listen for the song in your heart, those notes that strike a chord of truth remembered.

There is one thing more I must say. It is not only we who must awaken, but the sleeping world as well. Let's start singing the song the world is longing to hear. It is the song our souls remember.

DAILY DARE
Nourishing the Seeds of Your Soul

Today, consider three small ways you can make a contribution just by being who you are. What might happen if these tiny seeds were watered with your love? In your Lifeseeds Journal, record ways you can bring more light and love to these seeds you have too long neglected. Today's dare corresponds to the "Three Seeds of Soul" tool from the Lifeseeds Toolkit.

Lifeseed #8—Trust Yourself to Know the Tune

8

We dreamed a dream and lost our way, believing all was lost.
We forgot all we knew. Do you see it now? Close your eyes. Step into it —
that magical place rooted in your soul that you convinced yourself was
just a dream. This is what's real. Within you is an ever-expanding
universe where you can become. Listen to the song of your soul,
that singular lullaby that sings the world awake.

FOCUS TEXT
Lullaby

We start at the beginning, with the infant born into this world innocent and knowing, pure and wise. Let us imagine that infant inside of us. With a gentle compassion, reach within and cradle that infant in your arms. And simply begin to hum.

And then to sing. A lullaby. An anthem. A tune long forgotten. Here the magical mystery tour begins.

Trust yourself to know the tune and to sing the child in you awake. Ah, to see her whole and complete, her heart beating with the force of life. Each breath she takes a reconnection to the Divine from which she came. And as her eyes open, gaze down upon her with deep love and honor. Know she has come to be your teacher.

From this moment on, assure her that you will care for her. And as you realize she is gazing back upon your face, imagine what it is she wants you to know right now.

Hear her. See her. Love her. Let her be your guide. As you hold her in your arms, you will receive all you have ever needed.

LIFESEED
Trust Yourself to Know the Tune

Picture the baby you were. Did anybody ever tell you how your presence lit up the room? If you had the chance to be with that little child, what would the babe whisper in your ear? What is the song he would want to hear? What would still her and quiet her fears?

Whatever the song you learn to sing, bring these little ones, so long left behind, into your whole presence. See with the heart of a child all the possibility and know it is held safe, no matter your life's circumstance. The song cannot be stolen from you. This little child, held within you heart and in the arms of the adult you, will teach you all you long to know.

DAILY DARE
Inner Family Reunion

Today, picture yourself as a tiny baby. Then imagine you at three years old, at five, then ten, then sixteen and twenty-one. Shower all the pictures you envision with all the love you longed to have when you passed through these years. You are these children, and they belong to you. Each morning and each evening, tell each one that you are here and all is well. Then, sing a lullaby, trusting yourself to know the tune. Let your Lifeseeds Journal be a safe place where you shed light and love on any past wounds or hurt places. Celebrate your reunion with these pieces of you. Today's dare corresponds to the "The Inner Family Reunion SEA Doodle" tool from the Lifeseeds Toolkit.

Lifeseed #9—Welcome All into the Guest House

9

The sound and the fury raged. Afraid of being lost
in our own confusion, we became a perfect storm of strangers,
within and among ourselves, and turned the parts of ourselves and the
people and groups we deemed "other than" away, further separating
ourselves. To our surprise, we find that unity is born of diversity.
We welcome all and dancing the colors back into the light,
honoring and appreciating the gifts they bring.

FOCUS TEXT
There Is No Harmony without Resonant Consonance

Too long have you quieted the voice of emotion within you — both the laughter and the cries. Too long have you tried to tame the spirit of who you are, chastising the child you left abandoned in your hurry to grow up. You wanted to take life seriously and leave behind the frivolity of youth. Still, that child is waiting to greet you and throw her arms wide around you.

Some are tentative. Some are joyous. Some stand at the periphery and wait to be ushered in. Others race toward you with unbridled enthusiasm. They look up, eager to receive your direction, and when you see them you know what to do. You remember a place and time, in the world of physical reality or in the world of your imagination, where you felt safe and loved, as if you had always belonged. Go there now. Take the child you were with you. Show her the way.

Are you there?

Take in the sights and sounds, the miracles unfolding in every direction, coming clear right before your eyes. More than one child may appear. Welcome all. Sit together in a circle and know this: all is well. This is the point of beginning. This is the moment outside time, the place of unlimited possibility. Begin and begin again.

You are awake now, and in wholeness, you take your first breath, ushering in a new experience of what it means to truly live. Come together and live as one.

LIFESEED
Welcome All into the Guest House

At some point along the way, it seemed easier to just stay quiet. Fly under the radar. Keep out of the way. Maybe you did your best to manage everything that flew fast into your face, but life caved in around you. That's how you know what it's like to feel the Earth beneath your feet.

The child or teenager full of promise has remembered a place of safety for you. Even the ones who led you down a road from which it feels you cannot return carry the seed of a memory. Give them some voice to speak and trust the wind to carry all the pieces of you back together as one.

DAILY DARE
Imaginary Dinner Party

Today, imagine a party. You are in a beautiful home, spacious and filled with whatever finery and belonging that make your heart come alive. There is a large table. It magically expands each time a new guest appears. You go the table where a banquet has been prepared for you. You have invited all the noisy guests that sometimes fill your head and follow you in your dreams. Be present to all. Make room for a joy-filled reunion. In your Lifeseeds Journal, you may wish to draw a picture of seats around a table and give each "guest" or facet of yourself and your life's experience a place of honor. Know that you are all one, held together by the light and love of life itself. Today's dare corresponds to the "Imaginary Dinner Party" tool from the Lifeseeds Toolkit.

Lifeseed #10—Tune to the Vibration of the Holy "Yes!"

10

We are awake now. In wholeness, we take our first breath. We each find our unique frequency of love. With small movements of grace, feel the dance of life.

FOCUS TEXT
The Wonder of Seeing through New Eyes

Through the eyes of a newborn babe, you see clearly now the limitations you have believed to be. All is coming into focus. Time begins now to expand outward in ever-widening circles of trust. Trust in the here and now. Trust in what has always been. Trust in what is becoming even now.

And the feeling of your magical place is rooted within the soul. It is an ever-expanding universe where you can become. What's it like? Are there rainbows and waterfalls or a summer field? Are there butterflies and unicorns? Is your magical universe a scene right out of the Jetsons?

Whatever it is, smile. You have envisioned a world to which you will always belong. In the beginning, you were. In the beginning, I am.

Speak! Speak a soliloquy of syllables. Sing the symphony of you. Allow it to trickle down, to bubble up and then to cascade through your cells. Feel the vibration of this, "Yes!" and the resonance of the reservoir of truth welling up within.

Welcome to the world. With eyes wide open, your hearts will now become a portal to the truth of who you've always been. Bathed fresh in these embryonic waters of life, you will emerge whole from this time of endings and take your first breaths, your first steps. You will speak your very first words in a language imprinted on your hearts before time began.

From this beautiful unfolding, peace will multiply. Division will be no more. There will be no "other." Only the One. Only the dazzling sun and silver moon. Only endless sky with a billion stars. And a twinkle in your eye.

LIFESEED
Tune to the Vibration of the Holy Yes

Wonder — the very idea of it is something so many of us left behind, knowingly or unknowingly. It is, I think, no accident that as I write these words, I am sitting in a cabin in the middle of nowhere, and the name of that cabin is "Wonder."

Look fresh upon the circumstances of your life. More importantly, see beyond the surface condition and into the heart from which arose, at one time or another, a choice about how to see what was happening around you. The mind has fooled us into thinking only it decides. In fact, the heart of the matter is that you are a sovereign spirit who may choose at any moment to listen to those thoughts that present themselves or to simply notice them and allow your heart to decide your best course now.

Trust is a mysterious thing. We are accustomed to believing only what we see and what has been proven. Believe, and you will see. Perhaps, we have it backwards. See and you will believe, we say. Believe, and you will see. Dream yourself a world in which you are at home. Within you, there is truth. There is hope. There is light. Welcome to your world. Do you have eyes to see its beauty?

DAILY DARE
Imaginary Place

Today, consider the vision of your imaginary place. See all the faces that represent the whole of you gathered like a family. Keep this dream for you alone. Treasure it. Breathe it in slowly, deeply. Know you are safe and loved. In your Lifeseeds Journal, explore your imaginary place even further. Capture the detail of its wonder. Return to this entry whenever you are seeking solace from swirling negativity or anything that would distract you from the whole of who you are. Today's dare corresponds to the "Magical Place" tool from the Lifeseeds Toolkit.

Lifeseed #11—Be the River, See with New Eyes

11

Here on the shores of this new reality, we see with new eyes. We are awakening, if slowly, to the realization that all is not lost. There is a river flowing home.

FOCUS TEXT
Seeds of Recognition

We must learn to look at each other and see. Through the eyes of the soul, we must look for common seeds of divinity sprinkled in the soil of every human heart. Our first thought must be love. Love, like rain poured out on the parched field of humanity, collected and channeled into hearts made barren by lifetimes of neglect. We must awaken to this realization: all is not lost.

You underestimate the capacity of love. The love within a single human heart might seem a trickle. But when it is tapped to quench the thirst of one who has forgotten the beauty of its taste, it unleashes tumbling waters of grace. If you could see from here the coursing rivers and the swift current of change flowing now because a single human heart chose once love, you would not hesitate to surrender all resistance to its flow.

Be the river running through the other's dry and dusty heart. Cut right through deep canyons where a life's left echoing. Lift them up on wings of eagles. Lift them up so they can see their hearts of treasured jewels, a home for all who would fly free as one. Gaze upon them with such wonder at God's glory come to Earth.

Tend to them as little children at the moment of their birth, until they stand one day, majestic, triumphant, rising from the ash, smiling down upon the river, wearing life like colored splash of sun. Having lived lifetimes, they may feel because you smiled upon them that they have only just begun.

LIFESEED

Be the River, See with New Eyes

Cynicism is a sickness in our society. I know, because I lived with it. Everywhere I looked, I saw people out to get me, or nothing worth saving. The paranoia and the bleak, harsh judgments I levied in my heart space never led to safety or to joy. Instead, they slowly squashed my true nature, which is a state of trust.

Try this: begin every thought you think with love and gratitude — for you, for any other person, place, or thing, and for this world we live in for a time. Now, think whatever you'd like, but begin always with love. See how it changes everything?

It has been some time now since I began to even consider this practice, and, though I am far from perfect at it, I am astounded at the vastly divergent outcomes I have experienced when I manage to remember to see first through the eyes of love, to let my first thought be love.

I believe our world is going to be amazed at what has been here all along in the midst of the chaos and disorder. Underneath it all, there is love. When enough of us wake up that truth within, we will live again in a world of wonder. Try it today. Be one with the river of life. See the light and love at the foundation of all that is and will ever come to be.

DAILY DARE

Love What You Would Resist

Today, whatever the thing that appears to scare you, to provoke you, to exhaust you, or to annoy you, see it through your real eyes. Begin with love. Make note of what you discover when you do. In your Lifeseeds Journal, write about any surprises you find or truths you discover as you see with new eyes and look beneath the surface of things that so easily deceives. Today's dare corresponds to the "Through the Eyes of Love" tool from the Lifeseeds Toolkit.

Lifeseed #12—Choose to Honor Choice

12

We became so cynical along the way. Stubborn. Resisting life's flow. We wanted to have it our way, to live up to all the expectations we had, to change the world to suit the way we thought it all should go. We didn't really like the idea of honoring what or who we saw as a problem.

FOCUS TEXT
Allow What Is to Be

We come here with the remembrance of and the desire for perfection. And so many of us are roused to anger at seeming injustice when we see another suffer needlessly or stumble over the same roadblocks. A little thing we miss — our rage conceals the truth that those blocks are, in fact, often the direct result of our collective choice or forfeit of our right and responsibility to choose.

If we are not angry, we may become consumed with a grief so global that we lose our way as we mourn what used to be. Whether fueled by the emotion of anger or a deep, pervasive sadness, we go to work and work for change. We get into action.

To work for change is noble and just. Yet, neither blaming the other nor losing self to the deep waters of suffering leads forward. As we raise awareness of what is and lead the way for change in love, there comes a point where we must allow what is to be. In doing so, we need not conform our lives. Nor must we sacrifice higher ideals. There is a third thing.

We find one way through and forward in the roads you choose to follow. Live simply and simply live, allowing space for all forms of expression and experience, trusting others to make the choice to do the same. And if they do not choose to allow what is to be, choose to honor their choice not to choose. Decide to let it be, and be who you choose to be.

LIFESEED
Choose to Honor Choice

Why are other people so slow? Why don't they get it like we do? Why don't they get you? Why isn't anybody paying attention? Why doesn't somebody fix it? That's all we really want to know.

But these questions lead us to extremes that serve to keep us occupied in what we see as high and good, while in fact these are mere diversion from all that matters most. You see, many of us get busy doing what we think needs to be done and think ourselves the hero or we throw our hands up and surrender, resigned to join the crowd and float through life. There is a third way.

Live simply. Simply live.

Let it all be as it is. Apply your love and creativity to all that you encounter without the need to change it into something else. What's magical about this is that when we allow a space for others to choose and set out to choose the best ways we see to go, we stop noticing all the fault lines and broken people in our world. Rather, they change before our eyes and become, without changing at all, beautiful.

DAILY DARE
Make a New Choice

There is a choice that was made by someone somewhere and it seems wrong to you. Perhaps it wounded you, changed the course of your life even. It happened. Today, allow your choice to be a choice only you can make for you. Rise up. Walk on. Choose a whole new way of seeing this day as you honor your own life as it is. Live simply. Simply live. In your Lifeseeds Journal, write about the new choice you are making and the new story of your life you are creating through these choices. Who are you becoming? Today's dare corresponds to the "New Decisions, New Directions" tool from the Lifeseeds Toolkit.

Lifeseed #13—Be Here. Be Now. Be Now Here.

13

How did we get so distracted? So sidetracked? So busy working for something more and a better life someday, we forgot to look around and what was here and now. Having come full circle, we arrive in this present day, so beautiful.

FOCUS TEXT
Choosing Now

Freedom comes in choosing now. When we surrender fear, we cast off the illusion that giving more means we will not have enough. Love remains exponential in its reach. And if you are the only one then you are the only one.

Expand to fill the space. Or be the desert rose.

You've heard the saying, "Bloom where you are planted." Do not wait for the right time, for the right environment, for the right circumstances to fall into place. Be here now. Be now here. And, if you are nowhere, then be there and know you are loved. And know you are love. And know love. Know there is no thing greater than love. Love is there.

Always, there is love.

Feel it rising up within you in this moment. Believe it to be there in the other. Believe it with so firm a conviction that you can make no choice but love. Love one another. Love when there is no cause for love. Be the cause of love. Be the causeway. Give life a reason to believe. Believe there is a reason.

LIFESEED

Be Here. Be Now.
Be Now Here.

Essentially, we all want freedom, and most of all the freedom to be. Here. Now. Fully. It becomes a matter of trust. Do we think we have to have company to experience freedom? Do we think we have to break free of something first in order to experience ourselves as free?

The tiny flower bursting from the seed that fell between the cracks of the sidewalk does not take a look around and say, "Oh no, look where I am. Someone may step on me. I have no friends. My life will be short. Why should I bother?" No, she allows life to be and waits for the sun.

When we believe in life and seek only love in our own hearts and deep in the heart of another, we set ourselves free of a tyranny that it must be a certain way. You are free to choose, and I hope you choose love in this moment and the next. Let its current carry you back to the free spirit you were created to be.

DAILY DARE

See Yourself as Free

Today, in all the situations you find yourself to be, no matter how troubling or lonely or raucous or challenging in any way, consider the flower that grew from the seed. Become the seed, allowing life now, even in this presence circumstance. Choose now, here in this day, notwithstanding such circumstance, to know you were created free and are free to choose. In your Lifeseeds Journal, write a sentence that affirms a view of yourself as free. Record the choice you make to honor the freedom of your spirit today. Today's dare corresponds to the "Seed of Freedom" tool from the Lifeseeds Toolkit.

Lifeseed #14—Surprise! Get a Sense of Humor

14

We got so serious. Do you remember the pure joy of greeting the dawn? Can you hear yourself laughing? Returning to our joy, we laugh our way to life.

FOCUS TEXT
Where's Your Sense of Humor?

You trounce through your whole lives serious and dutiful and miss the punch line. You begin as little children laughing and, if others are fulfilling their purpose, your sole purpose is to play and to tap a deep reservoir of joy.

Sadly, many of you actually mastered this first class but were then misdirected by your own parents and certainly by society. You were told to behave and play follow-the-leader. Problem is, the self-appointed leaders were moving in small circles. It is truly funny to watch it from afar. But it breaks you. And that is no laughing matter.

See if you can go back before the dour deciders directed you on a path altogether palatable but bland and boring. Can you remember the pure joy of greeting the dawn? Can you remember when you knew, unequivocally and without a moment's hesitation, that life was a surprise every day? If you can no longer recall the feeling, let's play "make believe."

Now, some of you arrived here and were so awake upon your arrival that you were quite literally terrified of what you found in this place. Jolted into the reality that this life would be no picnic, you hit the panic button and begged with your very souls to go back. But there is no going back. When you're here, you are here. So make the best of it.

If you have been sad, give yourself a comedy hour. Every day. Seek curiosity. Do the chicken dance. Laugh out loud at this upside-down world spilled out like a box of toys in a toddler's play room. Insist on finding pleasure. Resist the urge to wallow in the plentiful pain. In short, get a sense of humor.

LIFESEED
Surprise! Get a Sense of Humor

Play. The very notion of it was lost somewhere for me. I have a vague recollection of these moments of bubbled laughter rising up from long-forgotten rooms.

I have been one jolted by life — gripped with terror at the slightest of moments. I imagine if you are reading this you may have experienced that at least once in your life. I am and you are here. The question is how can we enjoy life's ride?

Many of us have created lives, or felt them forced upon us, that seem to remove the possibility of life as "a surprise every day." In such cases, it is up to use to "give ourselves a comedy hour" and find a way to reclaim the joy for which we are created.

Wherever you are today, dance in big circles in the rain of your life. Spill out all your blocks. Look for laugh-out-loud moments.

DAILY DARE
Surprise Yourself

In this day, be present to the level of joy and lightness you allow into your life. Just be curious. Seek to amplify your experience of playfulness. Be open to life's little surprises, which show up in surprising packages. Write about this experience in your Lifeseeds Journal. Today's dare corresponds to the "Life's Surprise Box" tool from the Lifeseeds Toolkit.

Lifeseed #15— Live the Magic, Dance with Mystery

15

We have been so busy sending out our own SOS that we missed the silver lining. Do you remember how the clouds dance against the blue sky? We breathe the mystery, dancing back to joy.

FOCUS TEXT
Look Up!

If you need a little help, lie on the ground in silence and watch the clouds roll by. There's a free show every day, every hour on the hour and most any other time you take the time to see. Every morning, the sun comes up. Every night, the sun goes down. Clouds dance upon the stage of your world, shape-shifting and becoming.

Who says the only applause needs to come from the thundering heavens? Up here, we're content and thoroughly entertained. You seem oblivious to the magic and wrongly assume this moment is just the same old song and dance over and over and over again.

Take a second look. And a third and fourth.

Quick, there's a show starting right now! Want to catch it?

You never know what will happen.

LIFESEED

Live the Magic, Dance with Mystery

We are forever looking down. Some of us to be certain we put one foot in front of the other. Or to be vigilant about our safety. Maybe we are obsessively considering whether we are wearing the "right" shoes or headed in the proper direction. The danger in doing too much of this is, of course, that we miss the magic and the mystery.

Most of us mastered the art of serious or some pretense of it. Let's go back to class for a lighter fare. Life is a show worth watching. Go catch a show. Smile at life unfolding. It doesn't matter what shoes you are wearing or if these shoes are tied. The show will go on and it's playing now right where you are.

DAILY DARE

Catch a Show

Today, notice the shape and forms in the sky and springing forth from the earth below your feet. Find a show you like, one that connects you to the magic stream of mystery, and attend as often as you can. In your Lifeseeds Journal, write about the show you saw and what you loved about it. How did it feel to simply sit and watch the clouds roll by? Where did you see your own life reflected back to you in the wonder that unfolded before your eyes? Today's dare corresponds to the "Free Show" tool from the Lifeseeds Toolkit.

Lifeseed #16—Know You Are Loved, Beyond Measure

16

We've been stumbling over a truth hidden in plain sight. Message after message, wave upon wave of truth, rise up from within. You are love. Do you remember now? Love is who you are. We read this message in a bottle: "SOS: You are loved beyond measure."

FOCUS TEXT
This Is Your Message in a Bottle

The shores of your world are filled with reminders of how deeply you are loved. It's as if, in your lives, you are walking along a beach, literally stumbling over bottle after bottle, each capped and containing a precious message of assurance and protection. They appear one after the other, piling up layer upon layer.

And you never even bother to look down.

Few are the ones who stop and recognize at all that someone somewhere is trying to get a message through. Fewer still are the number among you who bother to pop the cork and read the message. It is rare indeed to find one whose heart is ready to receive the abundant truth.

SOS: You, as you are, are loved beyond measure.

There are endless oceans filled with wave after wave rising and falling with this resounding message. Let it wash over you. Let it change your world. I hope you're getting the message.

When you do, pass it on, ok? And pick up the bottles, will you?

LIFESEED
Know You Are Loved Beyond Measure

Someone's trying to get a message through. Urgently. Life is inviting us to wake up and pay attention to these love notes written in the stars and sprinkled through our days. Still, we walk right past it all, eyes fixed on some destination we deem important.

Your life's journey is filled to the brim with wonder. Everywhere you look you will find evidences of the ways your life is supported and affirmed. It's time to open the bottle and pour on some truth, then raise your glass and celebrate being here.

You are safe. You are whole. You are loved beyond anything you might imagine. How do I know? A little birdie told me.

DAILY DARE
Listen to the Waves

Imagine you are on a beach alone, just listening to the waves. See if you can hear them now. Watch them crest and then rush with abandon toward you. They carry an invisible truth in the sound of their breaking on the shoreline. Today, what are the waves wanting you to know? In your Lifeseeds Journal, write about what you hear inside you as you imagine yourself on the beach listening to wave upon wave, rushing into your heart. Today's dare corresponds to the "Wavelength" tool from the Lifeseeds Toolkit.

Lifeseed #17—See Life as Multidimensional Reality

17

Our way of seeing limits us. Discombobulated by direction, we played a game of opposites, putting up against down, left against right. Thinking we might at any moment veer off into oblivion and miss life. Yet, we exist within an expanding sphere of infinite possibility, all of it held gently in the container of this single shining moment of the now. Life expands to meet us on the way with an array of choices.

FOCUS TEXT
Discombobulated by Direction

You are accustomed to thinking of direction in terms of up and down, left and right. You see them as opposites. Go left, and you cannot enjoy the mysteries in the field to your right. Look down too long and the story goes that you may well lose sight of heaven and be doomed to a life dimmed by darkness.

You confuse yourselves.

You are only at the beginning. Human civilization has advanced at a rapid pace, and you live in a time of tremendous technological advancement. And, still, you see your lives as limited. You believe following a particular path will cut you off from what you might experience had you taken another way, so you hesitate and sit down at the fork in the road. Or you start off carrying the heavy load of fear and loathing.

Think of life as multidimensional reality. An expanding sphere of infinite possibilities exists in the container of a single moment. You simply are not equipped to see it, because you have been conditioned by defining descriptors of direction. You are not as lost as you presume yourselves to be.

LIFESEED
See Life as Multidimensional Reality

We play a game of opposites, end points on a line. Is it possible we are missing something, limiting our experiences as we see ourselves as insignificant dots on a fixed continuum?

How often do we think if we do one thing we are "locking ourselves in" and "closing off all other options"? You are, in this moment, the ever-expanding sphere of infinite possibility itself. In this day, you are free to see life differently.

Let go of all you thought you knew to be true of life and see where this freedom leads you. Start in the center of your heart with the voice of truth that rises up to remind you that you belong now to a world of wonder. You are sustained and cared for as you delve into the center and move to explore the edges of your life.

DAILY DARE
Explore Alternate Routes

Today, consider a destination on a map and all the many ways you might start at point A and one day arrive at point B — or a point we have yet to imagine. Hopping on the wide highway is not the only way to get somewhere. You may wish to think about the destination you have had in mind further in the pages of your Lifeseeds Journal. Consider the way you have assumed you would get from where you are now to this point of "success" you have imagined. What are the other possibilities? Today's dare corresponds to the "Six Ways to Sunday" tool from the Lifeseeds Toolkit.

Lifeseed #18—Open to Infinite Possibility

18

Bound by time, we think time has passed us by. Disillusioned, we feel the fire waning, lose hope. We see the flicker of time passing by, believing it's all going, going, gone. Up in smoke. Life raises us again to something more.

FOCUS TEXT
Up in Smoke

Sometimes, by the time you choose to be here now, you find yourself out of time. And all seems to be going, going, gone. Up in smoke.

Life passes quickly and much of it is gone before we even see the opportunity it presented us. Some of us arrive at a point of disillusionment. We feel the fire waning within us. We sense the flicker of time passing by. We see the sudden flash of all that has been left unsaid or undone.

Perhaps we lose hope. Perhaps we lose our way. But all is never lost, and the way is always opening up. Where we see the last ember, life rises up unseen from ash and raises us to greater possibility than we could ever have imagined for ourselves.

LIFESEED
Open to Infinite Possibility

Whether you are making time, doing time, or simply running out of time, there comes that moment when you think your time is up. Sometimes we spend our days waiting for some magic moment in the future or longing for the time that was. Maybe we don't want something to come to an end or we just long for a brand new beginning.

Time flickers. Hope wanes.

This is the moment in which we are met with the opportunity to trust that life will rise up to meet us. In the face of all your dreams gone up in smoke, open to the awareness that this, too, can be an opening.

DAILY DARE
Gather Evidence of Life's Recreation

Today, bring your full attention to the moment of this beginning again in your life. Take the 360-degree view, considering all the surprising ways you might find new possibility. Trust time to expand or contract as you focus on the seed of your desire. Stay present to the grace that is there to be found in the infinite moment of now. In your Lifeseeds Journal, capture the ways that you see life rising up to meet you just when you thought it was the end. Look over the course of your day, week, month, and year, and make note of all the evidence of life's re-creation. When have new possibilities emerged just when you thought things were over? Today's dare corresponds to the "Smoke Signals" tool from the Lifeseeds Toolkit.

Lifeseed #19—Be Found in the Great I Am

19

We see death as the final curtain, and mark time, mark, marching to the beat of the way we always thought it had to be. Yet, we are not found beneath a marker in the ground. We find ourselves and are found in the infinite unfolding of a life more abundant, a love without end.

FOCUS TEXT
Ashes to Ashes

It's not the end of the story. It's merely chapter one. We begin. Then, we begin again. And, while we have always seen death as leaving those whom we loved in this lifetime, we do not leave them at all unless we so choose. Our essence remains. The love with which we loved while here is carried forward.

We are not found beneath some marker in the ground that records the dates of our birth and passing to the new birth so neatly. We are found in the heart of the great I Am, the eternal birth, an infinite love for all that is and is becoming.

There is no too early or too late, no life extinguished. There is only changing form. There is no was. There is only is. What once was is now. You need not see the log on the fire to be warmed in this life. The physical is but one aspect of reality. Seeing is not the whole of believing.

We are here. Let your hearts beat with this truth. We are the lights that shine when you fear your light has dimmed. When your fire burns out and all seems lost, gone up in smoke, we rise with you to celebrate your awaited birth and rejoice in perfect timing.

LIFESEED
Be Found in the Heart of the Great I Am

Death seems to be the end of life, some final blow, like a tree chopped down. What if this were not the whole of who we are — this short time between our birth and our death, the thing we call life? What if life was something far more expansive and wondrous than the small box we've put it into?

What is the context you have placed your life within? How do you define who you are? Do you let your age define who you are? Where you live? What family you were born into? How much stuff you have acquired or the money you make? How many races you've run?

What is the larger world to which you belong? Where is the field farther than you can see?

This will be your home. It is now the refuge where you may hide beneath the shadow of winged ones. It is a home for your heart, and this home will not be seized when the body fades or the mind can no more remember all the ways of belonging you used to use to define the whole of who you are.

DAILY DARE
Write the First Chapter

Chapter One: You begin, and you begin again. Today, write the opening to the first chapter of your new life. Begin where you are, inspired by the light that is here for you. If you have lost someone to death, explore the idea that they are still with you in the pages of your Lifeseeds Journal. You might also wish to write about how your presence is with those from whom life may have separated you, for whatever reason. Consider the world to which you belong and the context of your life. Today's dare corresponds to the "Chapter One" tool from the Lifeseeds Toolkit.

Lifeseed #20—Surrender to Love

20

We feel loss, love, and all the space between. Then grace unfurls its wings, and we see clearly: We are winged ones, held in a wide embrace. A heartbeat from remembering, we are where love is to be reborn. Hope is not lost where love is found.

FOCUS TEXT
Grace Unfurls Its Wings

World without end, you are cradled in an infinite grace, an indestructible nest of love. Even as you fly far from it and fall from its comfort, love expands to hold you in its wide embrace. You are winged ones, migrating even now back to your native home. Rest in the truth that you have never been far away.

A heartbeat from remembering, you are where love is to be reborn again. Your life is the reincarnation of this truth. Love has not died. No matter your perception that all has been lost. Notwithstanding the darkness that surrounds you. Never mind the long stretches of shadow that have wrapped around the girth of your world.

Rekindle now the light of love inextinguishable. Hope is not lost where love is found, and love can be found — even in the vast expanse of space and time, seemingly emptied of all that is, yet filled with infinite grace and possibility. Surrender to that grace and you become love.

LIFESEED
Surrender to Love

Do you see yourself as the baby bird who fell from a high nest — or was pushed from its comfort? Are you the one who never quite found her wings? Do you think it's over before you really began?

Or maybe you know you flew far from all the comforts of home and left it all behind? Maybe you have never known a soft nest.

Here is the gift of life. You are still held within love. The spark that can light your life is alive deep within you. Surrender the need to make it make sense. Just let go. You will find your wings. Until you do, trust the wind to carry you.

DAILY DARE
The Angel, the Fire, and the Light Within

In every moment that arises, when you think it is all over, believe you have missed your chance and it is too late, imagine an angel appearing who will lead you gently into the center of your life. Sit by an imaginary fire until you begin to believe love is alive and you are the source of it all. In your Lifeseeds Journal, write about the idea of yourself as the source of love and also the idea that you are held within a grace that is truly infinite. You may want to do some doodling around this idea. Today's dare corresponds to the "Fireside Chat" tool from the Lifeseeds Toolkit.

Lifeseed #21—Observe Life Working in Your Favor

21

Certain of our demise, we reasoned it was coming to an end. The evidence that life held us, in the beginning and the end, was right there before us: in March lilies springing up, in rains falling down, in life springing forth.

FOCUS TEXT
Life Is the Cradle

Many of you have all you need but lack trust — trust that life is working for your good, always. Trust that you are loved, safe and protected. This condition has arisen from the instability you have experienced, usually as a little child. Let life be your cradle now.

Look around for the evidence that life is working in your favor. Observe nature and the natural condition. See how the March lilies spring up through the crusted snow. Observe and then participate in the dance of the changing seasons. See how life unfolds and provides a blanket of comfort in unexpected ways.

LIFESEED
Observe Life Working in Your Favor

Many of us, for a variety of reasons and in a wide span of life circumstance, lost faith in life a long time ago. We began, over time, to expect the worst or at least to give up the dream of a happy life. When we think all is lost, nature offers her wisdom.

As I write this I sit in the woods, where winter would convince us this is a barren world, brown its only color, silence its only sound. This is all my eyes can see. But my heart believes there will come a spring and my mind knows this to be true because I have witnessed the cycles of life in those woods.

DAILY DARE
Make a List of All Good Things

In this season of your life, track the comforts and joys that come in unexpected ways. Make a list and check it twice. See the truth before you in black and white and all the colors that appear. Life does not keep a naughty list. It bears all things, believes all things. Be convinced. Keep a list! Begin today. Use your Lifeseeds Journal to look for the good and invite more and more of life's favorable experiences into your presence and awareness. Today's dare corresponds to the "How Life Believes in Me Evidence Collector" tool from the Lifeseeds Toolkit.

Lifeseed #22—Unbind Yourself, Come to the Present

22

Squeezed by life, we felt divided into increments of time, boxed in, sliced to pieces. Here and now, weather or not, see the truth of who you are is undivided. There is perfection in each imperfect representation of who you are. We are free and see wholeness in every fragment. We are set free in the infinite grace of this very moment.

FOCUS TEXT
The Infinite Now

Being present does not limit your experience. It expands it to infinite proportions. When you bring yourself fully to the present, you open up entire realms of being and knowing. You gain access to immeasurable truths that can guide you in the next instant and in the very moment in which you find yourself.

Only when you are fully here can you be there. Or anywhere at all. There are ways of seeing time and space: the past, the present and the future, for example. Here, there, near, far — do not define yourself merely by such measures. Release now the illusion of limitation. There are no lines that cannot be crossed, for the line itself was created. There is only the value that we give a thing.

The truth of who you are is not divided into increments of time. The wholeness of you is contained in every fragment, in each imperfect representation of who you are. See yourself as uncontained, unbound by such delineations and descriptors.

LIFESEED
Unbind Yourself, Come to the Present

We are always worried about missing something. Especially in an interconnected world driven by technology. Pretty soon we are twisting ourselves with anxiety and tripping over our own feet in a hurry to make sure we keep up with everything there is to know and do and see.

We are afraid of being still. What if we miss our one golden opportunity? What if we never catch up? Now is the moment to all. Let go and allow yourself to be fully here. Now is your next opportunity window and you are free to free yourself from a way of thinking that places limitations on the wonder of your life.

Your value cannot be defined by how much you do or what you may accomplish in any given day. You are, in this moment, a whole world of wonder waiting to be born. Allow the becoming process to unfold naturally. Tend to the truth within you.

DAILY DARE
Create a Space for Stillness

Grant yourself permission today to sit in stillness and see your life in a whole new way. Meet yourself in this moment of the now and know nothing is lost. Your now will open in the room within your heart. Reflect on your experience of stillness and presence in the pages of your Lifeseeds Journal. Today's dare corresponds to the "What Came from Stillness" tool from the Lifeseeds Toolkit.

Lifeseed #23—Know You Are Well

23

Uneasy, we added too much definition, reduced to less than all we are, creators infinite. Stepping out of the illusion, we see all is well, and we are well.

FOCUS TEXT
All in All

You are all in all. You are all. All is well. You are well. See yourself as so, as having been and as becoming still. You are life, and life is you. Not just in you. Not just around you. You are not separate from all that is. All that is exists within you. And you bring it to its fullest expression. We can never fully capture all of who we are, for we quickly expand beyond the confining limits of mere definition. This is because we are a creative force. We are creators.

You cannot be reduced to the sum total of your experience. You are not the product of your past and present circumstance. You exist outside the equation of the future that you or others have predicted or envisioned for you.

LIFESEED
Know You Are Well

All in all, we have been taught to look for problems to be fixed, hurdles and hoops to jump through, and improvements to be made. We look for what we yet lack or how we might attain that next level of happiness — or even some measure of it.

We think we are this, and the whole world or some other with whom we are comparing ourself is that. We label and separate ourselves out so often. Sometimes, we look for pristine perfection, but most often if we find it at all we see ourselves as not yet belonging to it. So we strive to be better. Or we say our fate is sealed.

Get a new perspective. Try this on for size: you are whole. You are well. You are a complete dynamic and sustainable system of life held within a world of wonder and wholly belonging to it.

DAILY DARE
A Dialogue of Light

When something arises within you or around you that has you convinced you do not belong, envision yourself a spinning world whose radiant source of illumination is unmoved by whatever is swirling around you or within you. Allow the light and love to speak to you. Listen to what it says, too. If you wish, record a dialogue between the light within and you in your Lifeseeds Journal. Today's dare corresponds to the "Light Conversations" tool from the Lifeseeds Toolkit.

Lifeseed #24—No Mistake Can Be Your Grave

24

We labeled ourselves a "failure," empty, out of time.
We buried ourselves, hearts hollowed out. But no mistake,
however grave, can be your grave unless you so choose.
We mark the time by moving through it.

FOCUS TEXT
Markers

No mistake, however grave, can be your grave unless you choose it to be so. You are not at the end unless you limit yourself by labeling yourself a failure, a mistake. You are not that.

You exist outside the bounds of what result you have helped produce by right or wrong thinking. There may be a reason why, but do not allow that reason to define who you are, for it is only partial and not the whole.

So do not bother with the why. Focus, rather, on the why not. Knowing why something has been is useful, but asking of the present and future why not, rather than dissecting the why of the past, pulls us toward the recognition that we are always becoming more of who we are.

Mark the time by moving through it.

LIFESEED

No Mistake Can Be Your Grave

I know you have been thinking about it. It lurks in the corner, waiting for any opportunity to remind you how this might have been for you if only you hadn't crossed that line and thrown your life away. I know it because I have lived it. Do not allow yourself to be defined by a single moment belonging to the past.

There may be consequences and a river of pain. Let those be. Then, see: you are more. You are life flowing forth and finding a new way by awakening to the whole within you.

Why not dare to believe again? Why not move in the direction of a new meaning? Why not come to life again?

Should you be afraid of a disappointing end, why not walk in the way of the rainbow and see that you will be. Whatever the color of your life, you are a contributor to the everlasting light of love.

DAILY DARE

A Compassion Shower

Begin today with this practice: each time you think of that mistake in your past, give yourself a wide open field of grace. Open up a space to give and receive the love you needed then by connecting to its seed within you. In the pages of your Lifeseeds Journal, further the practice by recording a statement of compassion and self-forgiveness. Shower yourself with the gentle rain of light and compassion, standing beside the you you were with full gratitude, acceptance, and forgiveness. Today's dare corresponds to the "Coming Clean by Loving It All" tool from the Lifeseeds Toolkit.

Lifeseed #25—See You Are Inseparable from Love

25

Life can be devastating. It can turn in a second, and all is swept away. There are unexpected storms, the fire that rages on. Yet, Nothing can separate us from the love that is God or from God who is love. We will always be held in that love.

FOCUS TEXT
Weather

Life can be devastating. It can turn in a second. It can be frightening. It is always extraordinarily beautiful if we choose to make it so. We always have the choice.

There is nothing that can happen to remove this truth. No storm, unexpected turn of the screw, and no unforeseen accident or tragedy can separate us from one another as spiritual beings. Nothing can separate us from the love that is God, whomever or whatever your understand that to be, or from God who is love.

We will always be held in that love. We will always exist. That will never be taken from us. We may not exist in physical form in this world. We may not have the same capacity that we once had. Our lives may not look like we had thought they would or once intended them to be. We are. Love is.

LIFESEED
See You Are Inseparable from Love

What if a life storm appears out of nowhere and washes it all away? What about all the things you cannot control with the best laid plans? There is always the question of what if. It lingers and grows like a weed that chokes our lives. If we allow it to wrap around us endlessly or encourage it to climb inside our minds, it may well prevent our full flowering.

Weather is a fact of life, and it is always changing. This truth remains: the seed of life itself has never been swept away. The beauty that you are will survive life's most devastating storm.

You are. Love is. Always, you are one with love, and there is love for you.

DAILY DARE
Water the Seed of Light in You

Consider today the whole of your life, including all its storms. Notice you are still here. See how in your life, there is some tiny seed, a spark of life, that needs only a bit of love to begin anew. Today, water that seed with loving-kindness. Open to the light and love that showers down upon you and rises up from within you. Write about your experience with this in your Lifeseeds Journal. Today's dare corresponds to the "Umbrella" tool from the Lifeseeds Toolkit.

Lifeseed #26—Weave a Home of Beauty

26

Hopes dashed, we find ourselves again wanderers, searching for our home — for all we think we had or for where we always longed to be. We see ourselves as small, insignificant, the victim of circumstance. When we find the faith to weave again, the world becomes a better place. We begin to see we're not designed to cling to safety of obscurity.

FOCUS TEXT
Down Came the Rain

You see yourselves as small, insignificant — the tiny spider weaving its home in a quaint corner of the world. It is beautiful, and you are happy for a time. But then you see you have climbed up a water spout, and life's deluge washes you out unexpectedly. Again, all seems lost.

Rain or shine, you experience yourself as alone, displaced. Rain or shine, you shiver at the cruelty of nature, the twists of fate that require you to begin again. You feel you are always searching for your home and for what you think you had. You can't find your way back to that water spout that was the home you knew. All you can remember is the endless rain that washed out the dreams you had for your life.

But you are not designed to cling to the safety of obscurity. You are meant to weave a home of beauty. The sun may shine its rainbow light through the droplet of water resting in the crevice of silken threads that intersect the circumference of your new abode.

And up comes the sun. It shines down at the precise moment a child passes by, looks up and sees whole worlds reflected there. And that remembrance of the rain that swept your world away fades as new worlds are born in another because you found the faith to weave again.

And the world becomes a better place.

LIFESEED
Weave a Home of Beauty

Who among us has not had the experience of feeling that we were somehow out of place, caught up in a life not meant for us? When sweeping winds sweep away something to which we had belonged, however quaint that home might have been, we find ourselves swept away with that unexpected change. Though it has passed, we begin to see the storm as the one defining moment of our life.

To us, it is that thing that took all that mattered and left us floundering, desperately reaching for all the pieces of a life left in shambles — *that* is what matters. Some of us try to put life back in order. Others move on out of necessity but grieve what once was.

If we could see within the vast beauty of our renewal as we are born to the new beginning and knit together a life from what we have and hold within, we would not question life's beautiful design. Nor would we underestimate the grandeur of the human spirit that rises as a great bird and takes flight upon the wind.

Start where you are. Use what you have. Find faith to become the weaver of a new world.

DAILY DARE
Map Your Inner Landscape

Consider the landscape of your inner world. Paint a picture, literally or in your imagination, of the world you once loved and lost. Now, consider what was left after the storm blew through, whatever the nature or origin of your particular life storm. Finally, see what's there now and create a new space that offers inner comfort and some safety from such storms. This will be your secret garden, a sacred space that is a sanctuary for your soul. In your Lifeseeds Journal, write about a time you felt displaced by an unexpected life storm. Explore your decision now to weave a home of beauty. What does this mean to you? How are you creating a beautiful garden for your soul? Today's dare corresponds to the "The Secret Garden" tool from the Lifeseeds Toolkit.

Lifeseed #27—Feel the Tender Mercies of Becoming

27

We see our lives as compromised, our life less than what it could have been or should have been. Bewildered, we find our way back to the one undeniable truth of love and rest now in the unfathomable grace of second chances.

FOCUS TEXT
No Compromise

You may see your life as compromised, as something less than it could have been. Or should have been or might have been. But somewhere it is altogether possible that some beautiful soul may find the courage to fly again simply because you refused to curl up in the corner and drown in the tears you would have cried amid the devastation.

This is the pain of childbirth and the tender mercy of becoming. It is the miracle of conception and the unfathomable grace of second chances.

Love may come again to the world, and that love may come into being beyond your awareness and outside the depth of your field of perception. But because that love is come, humanity itself is healed all the more.

New life grows where once only nubs on tired branches formed to shield the few drops of sap left deep within the core. There, after a time, the passion of life itself stirs, gathering momentum, bursting forth eventually into a glorious spring.

LIFESEED
Feel the Tender Mercies of Becoming

When we dare to rise up, take our humble mat or whatever we have left in the wake of life's deluge, and simply choose life, we are not compromised. As we seek light for a single step in a new direction and dare to step into that light, not knowing where we will be led but trusting nonetheless in the beauty of life's unfolding love, we invite a miracle. The trick is to stay in the moment and feel the vulnerability.

It is far easier to curl up in the corner. Or to kick and scream, raging at life's injustice. We never know how our life becomes that light another may need when the life they knew is washed away without warning. You can't see it now: the full-forested life that may be when you plant the seedling in a field scorched by fire. Let yourself grieve, and then rise, rise to greet the new dawn.

DAILY DARE
Consider Your Options

Today, become aware of your many options in the light of where life seems to have deposited you. Consider them one by one, recording them in your Lifeseeds Journal and then choose to step out in faith, your face to the sun that rises from within. Today's dare corresponds to the "Into the Light" tool from the Lifeseeds Toolkit.

Lifeseed #28—Stand Amazed at Life Unfolding

28

Consumed by life, we wonder at the weight of its striking and sometimes terrifying beauty. Our results seem meager, and our lives pale in comparison to the heights of glory we had hoped to attain.

FOCUS TEXT
Beauty unto Beauty

These things are all connected. They began in the imperceptible seeds of faith, hope and love: in the potential, the perfection, and the wholeness caught up in the storm you could have called the end. Beautiful ones, you may never know when you choose to begin again what worlds of wonder might unfold, what beauty might be born from the simple courage you found to say, "Yes" to your life.

And, in time, when you are changed in an instant, the weight of this world will slip effortlessly from you. You will stand amazed at the good you have done and at the life that continues to unfold because you gave thanks for the breath of being and then gathered up all the strength you had and proclaimed, "It is enough."

Though your results seemed meager and paled in comparison to the heights of glory you had hoped to attain, you will see one day the cascading abundance that rushed out in every direction, infusing the world with the grace to carry on. Blessed are you. You may never know how many lights shine because you are.

LIFESEED
Stand Amazed at Life Unfolding

As we choose to begin again, we never know for sure how it will all turn out. We simply step out with the tiniest seed of hope, trusting life to catch us. We water that seed daily with what love we have. There, at the inception of change, where we take a leap of faith, we cannot see the beauty of the dream, for it is is yet to be born.

But as we step in faith and feel the wind lift us until we suddenly find we can fly, we are magnificent beings. When we see such courage demonstrated in another's choice, it takes our breath away and we are inspired.

Let your life begin as you give thanks for life and breath itself. Gather all you have and believe and see it is all you need. As you seek to rebuild a life of beauty, keep the eyes of your heart fixed upon it. Neither compare it to another's life nor to the world you see as lost to you.

Rather, let it have room to be and become. One day, when you are at home with making a home for the whole of who you are, you will receive the gift of sight. On that day, you will know the truth of just how much that life you saw once as small and insignificant changed somebody's world forever.

DAILY DARE
Count Your Blessings

Choose three things each evening that have been blessings on the way, recording them in your Lifeseeds Journal. Thank them one by one. If you cannot think of something, thank your life, your breath, and the beating of your heart. Listen for their song. Today's dare corresponds to the "All the Lights That Shine" tool from the Lifeseeds Toolkit.

Lifeseed #29—Dare to Take a Single Step

29

We don't set out knowing what's in store for us in this journey we call life. We carry a bit of trail mix in our pocket — something to snack upon. Then we see the road ahead. We doubt if we can do it, unsure if we are enough or have enough or dare to find a way. Do we dare to step into a new story outside our comfort zone?

FOCUS TEXT
Trail Mix

We don't set out knowing what's in store for us in this journey we call life. We carry a bit of trail mix in our pocket — something to snack upon. Sometimes that is more than enough.

Then, almost without warning, we find ourselves standing on a new frontier, on the line between all we have ever known and the field of our future. We see rivers making their way to a sea of untapped potential. Dreams we never knew we had appear on a far-off horizon.

In these moments, we may reach into our pockets for our meager bag of trail mix and convince ourselves we are totally unprepared and incapable of making such a journey into the unknown. And then some of us dare to take a single step in a new direction and find a mystery, a miracle and the full measure of magnificence contained within a moment.

Life rises up to meet us on our way, and we are surprised. Pack your trail mix, but fix your eyes on the way that opens up when you dare to step out of your comfort zone and into a new story.

LIFESEED

Dare to Take a Single Step

We want to know where we're going, to make proper preparations. We have learned to doubt whether these meager supplies are enough for whatever lies ahead. There comes a moment in our life's journey when we may become convinced we cannot make it. We cannot take another step. The mountains are too high. The flat fields roll out forever. The waters rise.

We are caught. We see the dream of daring the adventure even as we feel the fear of not having what it takes. We stand at a point of choice that might become our point of power should we dare to venture forward.

A new story awaits. The first step is simply to step into it, not knowing where this story will end and the next story begin. Life's adventure is itself the nourishment and fulfillment that we seek. Dare to trust in life, and step into the story you are creating as you move forward and beyond the horizons you have known.

DAILY DARE

Step into Your Story

What is the field of opportunity in your life? What story of you has yet to be told? How can you step into that storied field today? What will you do to encourage yourself when it becomes time to take a single step? Consider these questions in your Lifeseeds Journal. Today's dare corresponds to the "The Way That Opens Up" tool from the Lifeseeds Toolkit.

Lifeseed #30—Belong to All That Is

30

We long for belonging and so split ourselves into categories of belonging. In the reaching, we have all we need. We begin to see we belong to an infinite supply. We let it go and let it be.

FOCUS TEXT
Belonging

Beloved, you belong to all that is. You are that I am. I am that you are. You long for a deeper connection and a life of purpose, a place to belong. Be longing, then. In the longing for, you belong to.

As you reach for something more, know you have all you have ever needed. You belong to an infinite supply. So, let it rain and let it go. Let it be. Always know you are held within our love, as we are held within your hearts.

LIFESEED
Belong to All That Is

When someone else has assigned us to a category of being or told us where we belong, we often shrink ourselves to fit the space that other has deemed appropriate for us to fill. We may forget we belong to something greater and also to one another.

We long to matter, often in some certain way that happens to matter most to us. We want to know we count. These very desires held within our hearts will lead us back to the realization that we do, indeed, matter.

Modern physics tells us we live in a universe that is in fact comprised of many worlds and that all that exists expands infinitely. The things we see as fixed are often the things we think of as mattering. They are shape and form. They seem solid in the space. All these things are made up of the same atoms being ever arranged in new patterns of being. The energy that is invisible matters, for without it there would be no matter — no "stuff" to which to assign value.

We are all made of the same stuff. The same breath of being moves through each one of us. So long for all you desire to bring into your life. Know that no matter where another belongs, they, too, are longing for something. They too belong to life.

DAILY DARE
See Your Desires Coming to Life

What do you long for? Why does this matter to you? Write about how you can give yourself a taste of what you are most desiring in your Lifeseeds Journal. Today's dare corresponds to the "Life Desires Sampler Tray" tool from the Lifeseeds Toolkit.

Lifeseed #31—Allow Yourself to Be Broken Open

31

Unseen forces tore at our hearts. Love flattened us, leaving us scared stiff of life. We encountered love and pain along the way. Perhaps you met the image of all that was possible magnified in the mirror of another. And then it was gone, and you had no words. But love is neither created nor destroyed. Love remains, and we see we have come close to Love's true nature in our soul.

FOCUS TEXT
Trajectory

Many of you encounter a moment that is magical and meet the image of all that is possible for you magnified in the mirror of another. Usually, this occurs when you happen upon one you did not expect to find here, in this place, in this time.

Just as quickly as you found it, the magic disappears and the glaring lights come on just before you take the stage, blinding you. Or maybe the leading man or lady walks off stage, leaving you looking like a fool, standing in the spotlight wearing the naked look of love. Left with nothing to say, you freeze.

Off stage, you grieve as unseen forces tear at your hearts and pull you apart. Worlds are lost. You have been changed forever by the soul of another, in which you have seen yourself whole, at peace, loved beyond measure. What was given has been taken back, and nothing makes sense anymore.

It seems to you senseless that such a thing could be seized, held hostage or removed almost before you could catch your breath. Your hearts, after what seemed a single beat of wholeness, break now with their every beat. And, despite the purest desire to return to that place where you belong, life's trajectory, set by the free will of all involved, will not allow it.

LIFESEED
Allow Yourself to Be Broken Open

Life is full of surprises and people who do surprising things. On your life's journey perhaps you found yourself at home with someone. And then it was over, almost before it began. In their absence, you felt an ache.

You may have tried to make your way back to where you once belonged but found your way blocked. Life may have pulled you in a different direction. Or maybe the other person or people involved didn't seem to place the same value in the experience as you had. Whatever the circumstances that have led to a trajectory you did not plan to take, allow yourself the space to let it be. Release it gently, trusting life to lead you on to joy.

DAILY DARE
Love What Remains, Release What Is Gone

Think of someone no longer in your day-to-day life who mattered to you. Consider what you saw in that individual. What was beautiful? What did you feel to be possible while in their presence? How can you cultivate this good in you and tend to the seed, broken open and desiring new life? Take one action today to nurture the good and allow yourself to gently release what is no longer present. Capture what is revealed to you in this experience in your Lifeseeds Journal. Today's dare corresponds to the "Broken Open to Love" tool from the Lifeseeds Toolkit.

Lifeseed #32—Let Love Be the Fuel

32

Out of fire, we flew blind, feeling all was was contaminated, rendered null and void. We forgot that, even and always in time, day is always born of night. We became as stars shooting through the night, propelled by a mysterious grace.

FOCUS TEXT
Shooting Stars

Even though you see there may be no hope of restoration to your rightful home with the other, you circle round the dark side of the moon. You hold fast to that flicker of light, that singular moment when you saw your selves as once you were. Though one remembers and one does not, there will come a time when you shall meet again, your hearts collide to spark a memory lost to the one.

Carry on! Truth can survive the longest lie. In time, day is always born of night. Love remains untainted by another's willful dismissal of its shocking interruption of some presumed master plan. Ripped from the very love you've searched all your life to find, you fly blind on through the night afraid you will lose your mind. But it doesn't matter. Let the rise and fall of your chest be enough. Let love be the fuel that hurtles you through the loneliest years.

Let it go. Let all your love rush out before you to meet the void, and know this: love is never lost. Make your way, believing what gift has been bestowed will be returned tenfold, and what seems forever ending will find at last its new beginning. Have faith in beauty, and believe that you will rise again.

LIFESEED
Let Love Be the Fuel

When a star shoots across the night sky, falling through space and time, it leaves a trail of light. It is hurtling through the unknown, headed who knows where, and we, if we are lucky enough to look up at the opportune moment, gasp to see the beauty of its light. When we have lost love or belonging, it can feel as if the fabric of our being has been ripped from us without warning.

We scream without sound and may believe all is lost. We may think our very lives will end, and we will crash and burn. We may believe we will be reduced to nothing, lost in the void.

When your heart is broken and some life wound has been reopened, let it be. Let the love and pain flow as it will and fly on through the night. When the day seems long in coming, let love be the fuel, and let that love become bigger than what you first thought it to be. See that you and the love are one.

Live on, whether or not life leads you back to the one who was present when that love was born. Become the shooting star, burning bright, and know that the love that lies at the center of your being will sustain you through the loss.

DAILY DARE
E-Quality Finder

In your Lifeseeds Journal, list all the qualities you love in another. Seek evidence of these gifts alive and well within you, a seed gift protected from the loss you may have experienced. Allow this experience to create space for you to give equal consideration to the presence of those beloved qualities within you. The identification and appreciation of these extraordinary gifts of spirit within is a beginning to the full reclamation of who you are. Give thanks for this gift of love for yourself, and allow it to light your way. Today's dare corresponds to the "E-Quality Finder" tool from the Lifeseeds Toolkit.

Lifeseed #33—Breathe In and Be on the Way

33

We held our breath, waiting for the end, unsure of whether we were headed home or anywhere. Breathing in, breathing out, we were suspended in time and space. This is the home stretch, and yet a place of miracles.

FOCUS TEXT
The Home Stretch

Travel light. Good boots, good friends and the gift of solitude on an easy Sunday morning are all you really need. Breathe in that sweet whisper of a dream, and breathe out all that would keep you from believing in it.

Just breathe. And if you fall down, get back up again.

You are on your way, and you have come further than you think. There's a long stretch where the dust is kicked up and you're not even sure you are on your way home. In fact, you have almost arrived. You may think it's over. You may say there's no chance you won't be thrown out at the plate and lose the game for your team. Wait and see.

Do you believe in miracles?

LIFESEED

Breathe In and Be On the Way

We forget to breathe. It's that simple. We are so winded by the whirlwind of life that we begin to think we'd better sit it out. We're not sure we have what it takes. We may become consumed with a worry that we are not prepared for the road ahead. Yet, we will never make the journey loaded down with too much that is unnecessary.

Focus on the essentials. What is it you really need?

Begin with breath. Take in the beauty of your dream and release the fear that you do not have what it takes. Don't let a bruised spirit or a scraped knee keep you from exploring the way ahead. You have almost made it! The dust will clear. It's like the cloud of dirt kicked up when the runner rounds third base headed for home. He's not sure he will make it. He could very easily be out of breath as he slides into home, and there's no guarantee of safe.

In the stands of your life, there are fans you've never even met who are cheering you on toward home. Don't stop believing. Take in a deep breath, and say, "Yes!" to life's game. While often unpredictable, life offers rewards in *every* inning. For the love of the game, for the love of those who love to watch you play this game, and, above all, for the love of how you feel running the bases, running in the wind, get back up and begin again.

DAILY DARE

Just Breathe

Try this simple breathing exercise in the morning to begin your day. Breathe in deeply, and invite your dreams for your life to open your eyes to the way that will lead you closer to that dream. Breathe in energy for your life. Breathe out all that takes you further from the life you desire. Breathe in all the love that you may not yet see, trusting it is there for you. Breathe out all that would keep you locked in patterns of doubt and distrust. Know that within you is an eternal supply of love. Look for it as you move into the routine of your day. Listen for those who are cheering you on as you go. Write about this experience in your Lifeseeds Journal. Today's dare corresponds to the "Life Inspirations" tool from the Lifeseeds Toolkit.

Lifeseed #34—Dare to Believe in Life

34

Wounded or wounding, and sometimes both, we doubted our deservedness. Pulled back again to life's leading edge, we saw how we had been caught up in collusion, a conspiracy of silence and confusion. We saw how we had pretended to be mere ships passing in the night.

FOCUS TEXT
Double Dares and Life on the Leading Edge

How dare you? How dare you wound one who has yet to find her wings? How dare you take your reckless single shot and silence a song the world will never know?

And, you, sweet spirit, how dare you fall from the sky without a fight for who you are? How dare you lie there on the ground and forget you knew to fly? How dare you collude with one another and conspire to snuff out the very light that led you to where you are? How dare you?

Life dares to believe in you. Dare to believe in it. Come on, I dare you.

LIFESEED
Dare to Believe in Life

Life has hard lessons for us sometimes. One way or another, it commands our honor and respect. It is often more convenient to look the other way and just pretend we had nothing to do with whatever happened. We might point a finger of blame. Or, taking the opposite path, melt in a pool of inner shame. We may be tempted to call our life over because we think we deserve what happened. Or we may try to fool ourselves and simply push it back and say we've moved on to better things — onward and upward, never mind what was.

Make no mistake, moving past mis-takes and letting them be is a step forward, to be sure. But it is essential first that we take inventory and be honest with ourselves. We must take full responsibility for whatever part we played.

Life provides the space for us to be. Have we honored its graciousness? Or have we run roughshod over it, taking its gift and using it to take life from another in any form? Have we forfeited our right to love, joy, and peace in our lives just because we made an error in judgment or life took a turn we did not expect?

DAILY DARE
Your Second-Chance Choice

Daring to believe in life requires an honest evaluation of our beliefs, choices, and actions along with a willingness to forgive, beginning with full forgiveness for ourselves. To consider in your Lifeseeds Journal: When have you taken an action that dishonored life's gift? Have you broken trust by choosing a path where you failed to value your own heart or the free will and heart's desires of another? Choose again, now, love for your own life and for all life. Today's dare corresponds to the "Response-Able" tool from the Lifeseeds Toolkit.

Lifeseed #35—Choose This Day

35

In the deserts of our heart, we wandered, transfixed by life's unconditional gift of another way. We stood between forever and this day, pondering. We choose life and the promise of a new dawn.

FOCUS TEXT
Forever and This Day

On the one hand, it is true that you have all the time you need, forever and a day. There is no end in the way you have perceived it.

There is no hurry. There is only the one decision before you. What will you choose this day? What word will you speak? What reality will you create with the thoughts you think?

Will you choose to open the gift of the moment that comes to greet you? Will you remain oblivious to it? Or will you shove it to the back of the closet, hedging your bets that if you do this tomorrow will show up with something better.

Love what is. Live in the fullest possible way, into the gift of this moment. Like clockwork the days come one after the next, and you become accustomed to the ticking of time. And you never even know how sweet it is. Beautiful ones, don't be in such a hurry to get through this day and on to the next. Take your time.

Celebrate.

LIFESEED
Choose This Day

It is the simple choices in the moment that determine the experience we will have in the days that unfold and determine the composition of our whole lives. It is the course of those days that set the tone, tempo, and tenor of our lives.

The moment of now has arrived. It is a gift that is yours to open. Notice how you typically respond to the appearance of its gift. Do you shove it away and hide under the covers? Do you watch it appear with detached curiosity? Do you tear into it with ferociousness? Do you open it expecting a surprise, or do you believe it to be another trick? Today, notice how you dance with life.

It may seem you have forever or that it won't matter anyway, because your choices have been removed. Look again and see. Find the time you are given to be a gift. Unwrap it, and savor its presence.

Or, if by chance your life has lacked presents and you have seemed always out of time, stop and see now there is enough. Here and there are little moments of discovery that will reveal the true nature of your life as a life filled with infinite choice and gifts that lead you to a life more abundant.

DAILY DARE
The Question of the Hour

Every hour on the hour, or whenever you can in this day, stop what you are doing and ask: Am I thinking the thoughts I choose to think? Am I choosing the things I want to do? Am I living the life I love as freely as I can? You may even want to schedule this into your calendar or put a note in a prominent place to call you back to this question on a regular basis. Write about what you discover in your Lifeseeds Journal. Today's dare corresponds to the "What Now Infinite Choice" tool from the Lifeseeds Toolkit.

Lifeseed #36—Listen for Life's True Tones

36

Still, after coming so far, we filled the days with noise. Weary of attending the exposition of the fraudulent and the famous of the moment, we searched for a truth we simultaneously sought to avoid. We told ourselves truth had vanished from our world. Listening to the sound of silence, we hear with new ears.

FOCUS TEXT
Telling Truth in a Tone-Deaf World

Your days are filled with much that is unnecessary. You make much ado about nothing. You are bombarded with noise that clouds and confuses. You subject yourself and succumb to the onslaught.

There are those who speak truth among you, but you have grown hard of hearing. You tire of changing stations, of tuning in and tuning out to the turn of the trick. You grow weary of attending the exposition of the fraudulent and the famous of the moment. You search endlessly for truth and yet you fear both knowing it and not knowing it.

You see yourselves as jaded, jilted one too many times, left standing at the altar of confession. And so you stammer into silence, numbing yourselves with too much spice of life. Or you stimulate yourselves with sounds of static, silence, or smashing symbols, depending on the day — anything you presume might substitute for the voice of truth you alternatively seek and avoid. You tell yourselves truth has vanished from your world.

Listen. Really listen, and then tell me what is true.

LIFESEED

Listen for Life's True Tones

Noise. Noise. Noise. I am reminded of the Christmas Grinch who wanted to tune out the clamoring celebration of the season. And for good reason. Or so he thought. Yet, there he was scheming with noisy confusion multiplying in his head and cutting his heart off from what joy would be his. I love that Grinch; he is always teaching me.

Life is noisy, and we have learned to block out certain sounds. Meanwhile, we tune in hoping to find something worth listening to and are disappointed by life's same-old, sing-song song. Where is truth? We think we've missed it, and then in the next moment we are startled by it and reach to switch the channel or turn it off.

The true path lies in the middle, between a mindless overconsumption of ideas and opinions and that path that closes us off to anything new. We humans are curious. We seek truth, and then we bat it away. We say we want to see it to believe it, and when we do we reach to shield our eyes and cover our ears.

Listen first to both the silence and the song within you. Observe what sounds most true. Then, listen carefully with all that's true in you to find the tones that are most beautiful.

DAILY DARE

Make Music with Your Life

How do you cultivate an inner quiet? In the space you create for solitude, listen for what sounds true. When you find it, give that truth a voice in all you speak, in every choice, and in the music you make with your life. In your Lifeseeds Journal, write about life's truest tones as you hear them now. Today's dare corresponds to the "True Tones Melody" tool from the Lifeseeds Toolkit.

Lifeseed #37—Know You Are Safe in Space and Time

37

The terror of night became a holy gift as we counted the stars springing forth from our hearts. This river of miracles moved us at the speed of light toward the world we'd always wanted. Do you treasure that diamond of a star that lights your way?

FOCUS TEXT
The Speed of Light

    A billion souls have come and gone. Who are you to say that not a single one of them burns in midnight sky for you? Should you cross your arms, close your eyes and choose to walk alone, your diamond of a star that lights your way is, of course, lost to you. And the song you are meant to sing is swallowed up before you've learned its tune.

    You are safe. Uncross your arms, and open your heart to all you are deserving of just because you are. Practice this a little at a time until the day you can hold your palms open to the Earth, releasing any pain you have experienced and then turn them toward the sky to receive all the love you'll ever need.

    Stretch your hands out and touch the life of another who may or may not see you there. When you do, remember we do the same for you.

LIFESEED
Know You Are Safe in Space and Time

Do you believe that life is on your side? Or have you shut it out? Want to try a different way? If you just want to get off the fast track and move in the direction of a life you love and one that loves you back, take these four steps to freedom:

Step one: Tell yourself you are worthy of life's favor.

Step two: Let go of all the ways you have felt life's sting.

Step three: Open to receive all the love you'll ever need.

Step four: Be on your way.

Tonight, a billion stars will fill the skies. Tomorrow, the sun will rise and shine. What will you do, here in space and time, with this one shining life that is yours?

DAILY DARE
Let the Light In

Today, practice uncrossing your arms and trusting life to fill you with the experience of safety and belonging. Look for it today. Record what you find in your Lifeseeds Journal. Today's dare corresponds to the "Open Heart" tool from the Lifeseeds Toolkit.

Lifeseed #38—Be Free-Spirited in This Life, for Giving

38

Bound to a truth that trapped us or cut us loose, we made a new choice to refuse captivity. Binding up our broken hearts, we began at last to see life as forgiving and for giving, for free spirits all.

FOCUS TEXT
Forgiving

Life is for giving, nothing more. Nothing less than letting go will do. In this world and the next, there are those who would give their lives that you would be free. Among you, there are also those who would bind you to their truth — a truth they believe has already set them free.

Some know the harm they do, and do it anyway. Others have fooled themselves into believing they do what they do to you for your highest good. They have made themselves to be gods on Earth, blindfolding themselves willingly to all that is unfinished in their own hearts.

No matter your age, no matter your heritage, no matter your position in spirit or society, your soul cannot be bound without your full consent. Say you will guard your hearts and minds. Let no man make a prison of your body or take prisoner your soul. Refuse to be held captive by another, no matter how much you love them or how wise you think them to be.

Likewise, turn. Escape from all that would make you into a jailer of your own soul. Nourish body, mind and spirit. Neither starve nor stuff them. Neither repress them nor give the one free reign above the others. Make peace with who it is you are. Bind up your broken heart. Know yourself as the free spirit that you were created to be.

LIFESEED

Be Free-Spirited in This Life, for Giving

Sometimes we constrict the flow of life because we are afraid we are not enough. Worse, we feel sure we have to hold on tight to what we've got or it may be taken from us. We have learned to grab all we can and keep it safe. We are afraid to lose the little we have and afraid to give too much away.

It is true that there are those who would lock you in a version of truth not vast enough to contain the wonder of who you are. It is also true that there are those who hold a vision for your life as free. It is up to you which gift you receive.

Your life is for giving and may not be taken from you so long as you remember you have been born free, with a spirit of sovereignty. You may decide how to feed your body, mind, and spirit. Choose the best you can and allow them to serve you. Know you are a master who holds a vision for their full freedom. Give yourself the gift of presence and forgive all the times you have locked them away, afraid they might seize from you the little bit of freedom that you have.

DAILY DARE

See How You Are Seeing

What gifts of freedom will you bring to yourself today? Notice how you are seeing yourself and your life as free — or not. See the many choices you have in where you focus your love and attention. Exercise your free choice in all the ways you choose to be free-spirited and give to a life that is always giving. Make note of some of the ways you do so in your Lifeseeds Journal. Today's dare corresponds to the "See Free and Be Free" tool from the Lifeseeds Toolkit.

Lifeseed #39—Share Fine Gifts of Original Design

39

Born in ordinary time, we celebrate our origin and our originality. We see we have come bearing sacred seeds of essence, meant to be shared. We are awakening the world as we awaken to the world within.

FOCUS TEXT
Origin and Originality

We come from God, who is our home. Though we originate in the mind of God and in the womb of our mother, we come bearing fine gifts of original design.

You are no designer knock-off. Give up your search for some label, some stamp of approval. Set your own value. Declare your worth, and live as if you mean it. Make it clear you matter to you, for you are no victim of circumstance.

On Earth, we are born to parents and imprinted with patterns of life and spirit. We carry bits and pieces and are, in fact, immersed in the streams of soul shared with all of humanity. Willingly you gave yourself and gave of yourself, once upon a time, to take shape and form.

Now you are the maker of your life, the champion of your cause. Life is your canvas. What will fill your blank page, your stage, your silver screen?

LIFESEED

Share Fine Gifts of Original Design

You may think you're nothing special. You see yourself as average and ordinary, if that. Even reduced to something no longer relevant to the life that flows in the larger world. Maybe you look to the family into which you were born or the faith tradition to which you belong and believe you don't measure up. You think you don't fit in. You don't sparkle and shine like the chosen ones.

Yet, you come to this world with gifts all your own. It is extraordinary all the ways we forget this along the way. Here's the good news: now is as good a time as any to make a vote for you. You matter because you are here. Will you get it? Can you see it?

You came here for a reason. Are you ready to begin to share the gifts waiting within?

DAILY DARE

Beams of Light, Streams of Soul

How are you a true original? If you know, consider how you might let the light shine through you and from you to reflect that gift to the world. If you aren't sure about your gifts, ask your dreams to show you who you are. Consider all that you love and adore — places, people, and things. What do they have in common? How does this same stream run through your life? Make note of your gifts in your Lifeseeds Journal and look for new ways to explore them and share them with others. Today's dare corresponds to the "Origins and Originality" tool from the Lifeseeds Toolkit.

{2}
Life Reformation
for Integration and Flow

Find Your Forward Flow
A Whole New Way of Being Yourself

Introduction to the Life Reformation Journey

The Life Reformation Journey focuses on core connection to find our forward flow and reconnect to your essential journey. Together, let's connect to the Path of Soul Expression. The journey introduces you to a whole new way of being yourself. Think of the pathways or seeds for life below as invitations to further explore the territory of your soul and find your forward flow in your life and your life's work. In this second journey, we are remembering, **I AM LIFE**.

About Life Reformation Lifeseeds

Think of the momentum action pathways (MAPs) below as your living map and a guide for you as you further explore the territory of your soul and find your forward flow from the fertile crescent of hope. The pathways opened up by the seeds for life below correspond to the passages found in the second movement of *Cultivating Essence from the Matrix of Soul* and are explored in the book, *Finding Our Forward Flow*.

Seeds for Life from the Life Reformation Soul Journey

LIFE REFORMATION LIFESEEDS

40. REMEMBER THE DREAM WE DREAMED
41. HEAR ALL THAT WILL COME TO YOU IN SILENCE
42. RAISE YOUR VOICE TO FIND YOUR TRUTH
43. STAY CURRENT
44. ALLOW YOUR HEART TO EXPERIENCE CHANGE
45. KNOW YOU HAVE ALL YOU NEED
46. BREATHE DEEPLY AND WELCOME LIFE'S FLOW
47. HOLD SACRED THE FREEDOM THAT IS YOUR BIRTHRIGHT
48. SEE THE HOLY IN THE ORDINARY
49. CHOOSE YOUR MIRROR, SET THE SCENE
50. FLEX THE MUSCLE OF YOUR MIND
51. RETURN TO LOVE
52. OPEN TO FULL AWARENESS AS YOU LOVE WHAT IS
53. EASE INTO LIFE'S CURVES
54. STAY AWAKE FOR THE JOURNEY
55. FIND A WAY AROUND BLOCKS
56. BEGIN WITH GRATITUDE AND COMPASSION
57. GIVE THANKS FOR ALL THAT NOURISHES
58. GET IN THE STORY
59. FIND FAVOR NOT FAULT
60. CULTIVATE COOPERATION
61. SEE TRUTH WHEN IT SURPRISES YOU
62. TREASURE THE DANCE OF LIFE

63. LET GO OF A NEED FOR COMPENSATION
64. LISTEN TO YOUR BODY
65. KNOW WHERE YOU BELONG
66. LOVE YOURSELF FIRST
67. NOTICE HOW YOU ARE MOVING THROUGH LIFE
68. BALANCE WORK, PLAY AND REST
69. STAND IN THE STREAM OF YOUR LIFE
70. CARRY YOUR TRUTH IN GRACE
71. LISTEN FOR THE SONG OF YOUR SOUL

Lifeseed #40—Remember the Dream We Dreamed

40

Thirsty, we wandered through life's desert

in a never-ending quest, tripped by the sands of time.

Hot days, cold nights, and never enough. We forgot

the dream and the whole of we we are.

FOCUS TEXT
The Dream We Dreamed

There once was a dry land, parched desert, with the dusty particles of a dream that had died blowing about in the void. There once were a people wandering — nomads, thirsty and longing for a life they could no more recall. Burned beneath a blazing sun by day, shivering beneath the cold of night, they survived day to night to day. Always walking, stumbling, tripped by the sands of time. Delirious and waking to a common dream of an ocean oasis, they continued on a never-ending quest for something they had forgotten.

Until the day they died to lack and drank their fill from an abundance of stars smiling down upon them. And, in an instant, out of nothing, flowed a river. It sprang forth from nothing but a single choice to believe in goodness. The ground gave way to the expression of what they imagined. And then: a miracle. One river became two, and two became four. And four became sixteen. And the land became as fertile as their hearts.

This was the dream we dreamed and the way, once, we walked upon the land. And now the whole Earth is curled up, like a tiny infant inside each one of us. Eyes closed but becoming more and more aware, both of her grounding in a Universe far greater than herself and also of her own life and skin, she begins to flex her muscles. Her heart beats with the desire to soar.

Mother Earth is waking. We must hold her now. We must soothe her with our song. When she wails, care for her. When she cannot seem to rest, sit by her side. Thank her for the gift she brings. Share with her the treasures of your heart, the ideas that come to your mind. Remember the dream we dreamed, and give back to her, with gratitude for all she has given to you.

LIFESEED
Remember the Dream We Dreamed

Once you were, or perhaps even now you are, wandering, thirsty, seeking something to make it all okay. Somewhere in your life's sphere, right now, if you choose to see, there are stars smiling down. Here's the miracle: when we fix our eyes on what is abundant, no matter the desert in which we find ourselves, abundant rivers spring forth. The good is multiplied and magnified.

When we connect to the reservoir of truth held within our hearts, everything changes before our eyes. Life desires life, and when we choose to turn toward it, however small its presence in comparison to all we think we lack, more and more life emerges.

Consider the possibility that you bring life to life. Our interior world holds the seed of a whole new dream for our own lives and for all of humanity. Give thanks for all the dreams you've dreamed, then choose to see stars smiling down upon your life. Look for the miracle.

DAILY DARE
See the Gracious Good

Each morning, when you open your eyes, notice the abundance all around you. See what good life brings to you naturally and graciously. Each evening, count the stars and all the blessings of your life. Record as many as you can In your Lifeseeds Journal. Today's dare corresponds to the "Starry, Starry Night" tool from the Lifeseeds Toolkit.

Lifeseed #41—Hear All that Will Come to You in Silence

41

The sun so bright, we shielded our eyes
and encircled ourselves and each other with so many questions.
Unaccustomed to mystery, in a land flowing with milk and honey,
still we saw ourselves as starved. All the same, we stopped
reaching. Most of all, we forgot the source of our silent spring
and the rivers of hope that flowed forth from within. Then,
in a rare moment of silent reflection, the flood of truth.
Unmasked, we understood.

FOCUS TEXT
Reaching for Rivers of Hope

Remember the little kid running through the city, following the red balloon? Be like this child. As you keep focused on the goal of waking up, you will attract greater visibility. People will see what you are chasing after. As more of you focus on that red balloon, momentum will shift. Feel the joy of jumping up for that elusive promise. It will lead you to all you need to find.

There are layers within layers of awakening, rivers that lead deeper and deeper. These multiplied rivers will spring forth from your hearts. Your heart is the source of the source from which love and life flow. As more and more of you open your hearts, miracles will spill out, creating an ever-increasing flow of abundance. The rivers are an unfolding promise of pathways to joy, bubbling brooks to remind you of what you have always held within your hearts.

You see, the desert you have wandered in is the true mirage. And, too, as a people you have become accustomed to shielding your eyes and stumbling forward, chasing after all that has seemed so illusive. And there it is! Stop. Stop the endless search. Breathe. Breathe more deeply. Be still and know. You know what you know when you need to know it, and this is the time to know. There is no more quest, and your questions need no answers.

Ssshhh. Hear all that will come to you in the silence. In the sweet surrender to the here and now, you will embrace the mystery of all time. In the slow breathing in, you will find the fragrant flowering of your dream. And as you close your eyes, you will see for the first time the wonder of this world and be filled with the need for nothing more.

In the experience of this moment flowing into the next, your faith that this is indeed possible will spring a river of hope from which will flow a tumbling waterfall of love, bringing healing and new growth where you thought all had died. And from these buds of promise, passion is reborn. And through it all, you will know beauty. You will recognize yourselves anew and see yourselves grow into the full beauty of who you have always been.

LIFESEED
Hear All That Will Come to You in Silence

Faith. Hope. Love. These things remain. Though you thought them swept away in the wake of empty promises and a life of unfulfilled dreams, these seeds of beauty are yet present within. Rivers of grace and streams of the soul's truth flow through you, even when life feels dried up and done.

Reach beyond the break through this void for something that brings you joy. Think of the little child, curious, day after day, jumping up to retrieve a red balloon that drifts always just beyond his reach. The boy saw the balloon day after day and never tired of following it patiently, allowing in the joy of watching it dance in the wind, not needing to possess it.

Allow the silence to lead you to your red balloon, Nurture the tender seedlings in your heart — too long neglected, because you thought this desert time meant it was all over.

DAILY DARE
Delight in Your Life Today

What's your red balloon? What seems elusive and out of reach that would bring your heart joy? Consider something simple you love simply for the love of it. How can you delight in your life now, and how can you follow that desire more and more? Consider this question further in your Lifeseeds Journal. Today's dare corresponds to the "99 Red Balloons" tool from the Lifeseeds Toolkit.

Lifeseed #42—Raise Your Voice to Find Your Truth

42

We found our hope and lost it ever so quickly as life's winds shifted. We saw that we had fallen and felt we could never do enough. We could not find our way to truth and hope against such currents. We stopped our singing that seemed only a din of confusion.

FOCUS TEXT
Ebb and Flow

In every fall, there is a rising — the seeds of momentum that lie within, the gathering up of all that has survived the brutal winds of change. And, then, there is a moment of turning and, eventually, the swift influx of pure, essential life force.

When we surrender to that life force, once again we throw our arms wide open and lean into possibility. We allow the wind to carry us until again the time seems right and we find our legs beneath us and set a course for ourselves in the direction of another Spring. There is an ebb and flow.

You become like a chorus of frogs singing in the swamp of the unknown. They croak out of the simple conviction that they are and that conviction rises through the fog of confusion. Each voice is distinct and yet expanding in an echo of unity that rises through the long night.

Raise your voice to find your truth, and soon the truth itself will reverberate within you and lead you forward. The croaking will become the song of beginning again. Your voices will sound out together.

Together, you will awaken the new world.

LIFESEED
Raise Your Voice to Find Your Song

Life is a current that fluctuates, sometimes in an unpredictable manner. Trying to control its tides is a lost cause that leads to frustration and disappointment. What we can do always is to draw upon all we hold within and voice the song that lives in our hearts at any given time, and in any given circumstance.

When you speak, allow your words to flow from the endless pools of soul that reside within your being. You may not think they are there. Allow yourself to reach deep and dare to listen for your own song.

Begin to notice as you speak what words sound most true. We change our lives and our world as we contribute our essential strain to life's ever-evolving symphony. All notes upon the scale and instruments that vary widely are needed for the masterpiece to be complete. Let your life be one voice in the symphonic wonder of humanity.

DAILY DARE
See You, Living Your Dream

Today, notice the words you speak and those you hear ringing that you do not give expression. Consider what desires to be expressed through you. Explore one of these areas more deeply in your Lifeseeds Journal. Write about your dream in this area of your life. See yourself living that dream, writing in first person, present tense, about the experience you most desire. Commit to a single action that supports this vision you wish to create for your life. Today's dare corresponds to the "The Dream Alive" tool from the Lifeseeds Toolkit.

Lifeseed #43—Stay Current

43

We resisted change, having learned to fear what might come next. We pulled against the tide, clinging to the shores we knew, and denying life's current, for experience seemed a cruel master.

FOCUS TEXT
Staying Current

Imagine a river. Floating, you have passed the sudden bend. Ahead you see yet another twist in the winding river's course. You are not looking back, not anticipating. Just staying with the current. And allowing your self to be carried forward naturally, laughing with the joy of the river's flow.

You may have been told, "Don't make waves." But you do make waves. You are meant to make waves, because you are, in fact, a wave. You are dancing light, moving through space and time, expanding, changing shape and form, always becoming.

Stop holding back. Stop pulling against the tide. Stop clinging to the shore. Stop resisting letting go. Say yes to the unknown that is far on a distant horizon and rush into it. Life is here. Life is having kissed the shore and allowed your self to let go to be pulled back into a vast ocean of experience.

LIFESEED
Stay with the Current

Because we have learned life always has another surprise, and that there may be a fork in the road ahead that will change the experience of our life, some of us cling to those people, places, and particular things we most love. We only want something to be safe and sure. But life is about change, and we must adapt to its flow.

We ourselves are a pattern of change. At our most basic state, we are energy — a current flowing through this life. Consider this: your very life is a dance of light upon the stage of this world. We have become blind to this, believing life happens to us. We have dismissed our own value and deemed ourselves unworthy of life's gifts. Others of us, tiring of the changing circumstances have withdrawn our energy from life.

Let the tides of life carry you into something more. Begin by staying current and present to the wonder of change at work in your life.

DAILY DARE
Life's Winding River

Draw a winding river on a blank sheet of paper. Imagine this river represents your life. Where were the twists and turns? What were the rapids you nearly did not survive? Where will this river lead you? What is the current where you are right now? Keep your drawing in your Lifeseeds Journal and consider the gifts that are yours as you stay with the current. Today's dare corresponds to the "Currents" tool from the Lifeseeds Toolkit.

Lifeseed #44—Allow Your Heart to Experience Change

44

We chose duty and obligation, sweeping love's unpredictability aside. We convinced ourselves, we were in control, collecting impurities and debris that covered all that mattered most. Seeing we had been hardened by life, still we resisted change.

FOCUS TEXT
Distillation

Clouded by chemistry of obligation, the elemental essence of love has gone into hiding. Distillation is in order. But you must consent to allow your heart to undergo this change. You must find within you, individually and collectively, a willingness to endure the flame, allowing the release of toxins and impurities that have too long polluted the waters of your world.

Allow this purifying fire. Surrender, and know that your essential self, undivided, purest properties protected, will remain. Quintessential selves restored, you will return again to your natural state of being and cultivate from the core the seeds of soul that hold the promise of potentiality.

LIFESEED
Allow Your Heart to Experience Change

We look at our lives and see all we think we must do. We have promises to keep. We must work and eat and care for those for whom we are responsible. At times we are required to abide by someone else's rules. In all the responsibilities and obligations we feel, we often forget what is there for our full experience of life. It is right there, within us. In each one of us, it finds its unique expression.

Search your heart, and look for what is original to you. If you find, as many of us do, your heart is a mystery, perhaps hardened by events that crushed dreams or caused a deep gash within you, be willing to be willing to open to the process of change. There is much that clouds your vision and clutters the life within.

Are you willing to let life's fire burn away what no longer serves to reveal all that is most true? Trust is required, and to dare to open one's heart to change is no small matter. Yet, the reward is a whole new experience of who we are—one that is richer, deeper, truer. As we are restored to our natural state, life will show up differently, because we are changed from the inside out.

DAILY DARE
Consent to Change

Each day, consider your level of willingness to open your heart to change. Ask: am I willing to be willing to allow life in? Will I dare to consent to allow change to unfold within me? Write these questions and your response in your Lifeseeds Journal, then sign your consent to change. Today's dare corresponds to the "Life Change Consent Form" tool from the Lifeseeds Toolkit.

Lifeseed #45—Know You Have All You Need

45

We thought it was too late to dream, to dance,
to love again. We stood in a glorious field, frozen and feeling
hollowed out. If only someone might pour in us a blessed balm.
But then, where would we go? How could we
move in this hard shell?

FOCUS TEXT
Maybe You're Just Rusty

Worn out, beaten down, you can see you're in a field of dreams. But you don't know how to move or which direction to take. You think you've lost your heart, because you've lost your way.

You've become the tin man, stiffened by circumstance, feeling, perhaps, hollowed out by having lost your chance to cast off all your cares and dance your way to where your heart has always longed to be. But maybe you're just rusty. And maybe you have all you need.

LIFESEED
Know You Have All You Need

Often, we may look around and see the wonder of life unfolding outside our window, and still we think we have missed the boat. Our present circumstances or the way we feel may lead to a belief that freedom and change are simply no longer possible. We think we are hopelessly adrift, lost in the sea of our lives.

We reach a false conclusion, believing our hearts are beyond repair, much less restoration to the whole that once existed there. We give up on ourselves when we forget to begin with what may be covered up but can never be seized or taken from us. All that is essential remains within. Our hearts have simply become sealed with all the rust that has accumulated in our absence.

Isn't it worth more careful consideration? Let life loosen all that has become lodged in your heart. Trust that all of who you are and all you will ever need is there, waiting for the day it can be poured out on your life again.

DAILY DARE
Letter of Love

On the days you awaken and feel you cannot move, much less dance your way to freedom and full expression, be with your rusty life. Open your heart, envisioning the river of life within you. Trust the day to hold you. Believe you are enough. Today, in your Lifeseeds Journal, write a letter from your soul to yourself in your present human experience. Express your presence, love, hopes, and dreams for your life. Today's dare corresponds to the "Love Letters" tool from the Lifeseeds Toolkit.

Lifeseed #46—Breathe Deeply and Welcome Life's Flow

46

We believed we stood in the field alone, forgotten by life. We created perpetual stories of lack and missed life's abundant flow. Our breathing was labored, shallow, and we took all we had for granted. Stuck, we were alive but barely breathing.

FOCUS TEXT
Breath

The thing is, you can choose to change your life in every breath in and in every breath out. Breathe in spirit. If you don't inspire you may well expire in one form or another, so just breathe. Okay? Breathe in the assurance that you are not alone but are instead intimately and infinitely connected to all that is. Breathe out all that would keep you apart from the truth of your essence.

Deep, focused breathing will take you back to truth. Practice it. Follow it. When the sun rises, give thanks with your breathing and welcome the day. When the sun sets, allow your breathing to return to grateful appreciation. Give thanks with the rise and fall of your chest and know that you have all you have ever needed and all you ever will.

Allow your body to open fully to your breath, expanding to welcome the flow of life. Feel it fill each chamber up and then move deeper within you. Expand as a balloon, filling the throat and chest, then allowing your breath to fill your mid-section and move down and down into the base of your spine and the root chakra. Feel the wonder of life with every breath. Take not one for granted.

LIFESEED
Breathe Deeply and Welcome Life's Flow

Breathing seems to be the most natural thing we do in this life. Yet, if we have been wounded deeply, it can be among the most difficult. We become, without knowing it sometimes, afraid to breathe. We are wary of life, remembering the carefree moments interrupted by tragedy or another's abuse of our tender hearts, our fragile bodies, and our pure minds. Or perhaps a memory of when we have betrayed life or wounded another lurks in every breath, and we already feel we take up too much air.

The breath itself heals. Each and every breath in can be a renewal and a cleansing. Nothing we have done or could ever do can separate us from the life-giving nourishment of inspiration. We are deserving of it and our deep replenishment by breathing in deeply will never diminish what is there for others. There is an infinite supply.

As we allow ourselves the space to exhale, letting out all that we do not wish to carry, we open up a space for life's spirit to stir within us. Let the breath of life fill you completely. Allow this simple experience of breathing to connect you back to you.

DAILY DARE
Noticing the Breath of Life

Notice how you breathe. Do you breathe deeply? Or are you accustomed to restricting the flow of life and breath through you? Explore the idea of breath and the breath of life in your Lifeseeds Journal. Today's dare corresponds to the "Breathing Space" tool from the Lifeseeds Toolkit.

Lifeseed #47—Hold Sacred Freedom that Is Your Birthright

47

The pain became so great for some of us

that we propped ourselves up as gods, splitting one glorious

kingdom of grace into pieces and claiming them as our own,

dividing humanity into smaller and smaller fragments

to which only a select few belonged. We sacrificed a freedom

freely given on the altar of a shallow success.

FOCUS TEXT
Born Free

We enslave one another and ourselves when we create false hierarchies and prop ourselves up as gods and rulers of kingdoms of our own creation. There is but one kingdom, and it exists for all in the present.

There is but one creation, connected as a whole and magically sprinkled throughout the Universe in a million special varieties. We are born equally free, created from the same stuff, no one any more special than the other.

If we are born free, then we are meant to live free and to uphold the value of freedom. The Creator and the creation call us to honor and protect the sacred freedom in which and for which we are created.

How are you doing with that?

LIFESEED

Hold Sacred Freedom That Is Your Birthright

We believe we must build a fortress, a tower, a kingdom in which we become the protector of all we fear we might lose. We see this life as a dangerous place and rush to defend our small space. In thinking small, we create a world of silos.

Equally free, we come from a common source. Yet we arrive in a world where most who share the space with us have forgotten they are free. And so they, and we when we forfeit the freedom that is our birthright, become warriors or jailers, knights in shining armor or dragons breathing fire upon any who dare to come close. If we are to taste freedom, it begins with our willingness to see ourselves as free and give up the need for building castles and walls around our hearts.

DAILY DARE

Reclaim Your Birthright of Freedom

Consider the feeling of freedom. See how easy that was to tap into something you think you do not have? As you move through this day, reach inside and reclaim that feeling. Freedom is given, because you are deserving of it, no matter all the times you have betrayed it. In truth, we are inseparable from the free spirits we came to be. You are born free. Live free. Today, in your Lifeseeds Journal, commit to one way you will live free. Today's dare corresponds to the "Four Freedoms" tool from the Lifeseeds Toolkit.

Lifeseed #48—See the Holy in the Ordinary

48

We lost our way. The flame gone out, we grieved at the fragmentation and thought it all too late. We lost sight of all that was gifted in lives we saw as ordinary. We saw the trapping of success and felt it was too late for freedom's ring in hearts weary of this world.

FOCUS TEXT
Retrieval

If you have lost your way or lost sight of the full flame of freedom, all is not lost. The way back is to see the holy in the ordinary. In fragments of time and in the people passing by, look for the miracle. Believe and seek to see again. Your sight will be restored as you recommit to acts of soul retrieval that begin with simple observation.

Two minutes a day can lead you into ten and then you will find an hour has passed and your heart has been held in harmony with the hallowed Earth and heaven has come closer than you ever knew it to be. And the free hours will be magnified into days and then sweeping vistas of freedom unfolding to infinity.

Retrieval begins with a single choice to reach within and reconnect with a core essence you may not at first remember. Trust that it is there. Listen to the stillness. Be with you without the trappings of the life you think to be free. Release them all and come fully present to all that is unknown. Know you are, and soon you will begin to understand who you are.

LIFESEED
See the Holy in the Ordinary

It may be that our connection to the freedom we were created to be has been weakened. To rekindle its flame in our hearts, we need only look upon all that is before us. In all the little pieces, the moments as they pass, and the people milling about, see what your soul would invite you to see. Simply be present and let go of all you thought you knew.

Return to the time before you decided where you fit in the scheme of things. Allow yourself for just a time to set aside all your preconceived notions of what this life is. Invite the you that is most true to lead you on a journey to reclaim a way of being present to your life that is consistent with an experience of freedom.

Reach within. Become aware that you are here in the midst of all of this. Allow that to be extraordinary. Listen for the invitation into a life flowing free.

DAILY DARE
Find the Beauty Beneath the Pain

Take two minutes to be. Simply bring your attention to what is unfolding in the life around you without need of recant to it or rushing to stop it. Look for the beauty beneath the pain. Seek all that is whole and complete within the broken things. In your Lifeseeds Journal, write what wholeness you find in what you had previously seen as broken. Today's dare corresponds to the "Freedom's Treasured Jewel" tool from the Lifeseeds Toolkit.

Lifeseed #49—Choose Your Mirror, Set the Scene

49

Caught up in the drama of our lives or lost within its plot, we felt a sense of hopelessness and despair. Our minds numbed to the predictable soundtrack, and our hearts hardened at the narrowed loop of our choices. We forgot we could get up from our seats and call the scene and change our whole life's experience.

FOCUS TEXT
Flix

What if it were just a movie? What if everything you saw mirrored in reality was playing out on a big screen? Because it is. For your entertainment.

Did you forget that only you decide whether to redeem your ticket for the show? Maybe it's time for some new movies.

Let's go old school and start with the talkies. Or, better yet, let's go back to before the soundtrack put our minds to sleep. The essential artistry of silent movies was in capturing the range of human motion and emotion, frame by frame by frame. Now, your movies are a blur, as if you couldn't get enough in real life. Let's rewind. Let's go reel to real.

Back in the screening room, much as we up here might like to edit the "reality," you are the producers of your lives. You direct the actors on your stage. You choose your own soliloquy. You choose what play is to be or not to be. You call, "Action!" and set things in motion. You choose when to call the scene or do another take.

LIFESEED
Choose your Mirror, Set Your Scene

When we really begin to pay attention to what is happening right there in our field of awareness, we may begin to notice so many things reflected back to us. Sometimes, we can see we have been living in a house of mirrors, our own distorted truths mirrored back to us. Try this experiment: change what you are looking for. Set the stage for the free spirit you decide to be.

Appreciate the wonder with which our lives have unfolded and all the experience which has unfolded so that we might better know ourselves. It is possible that we have missed the movie of our lives, taking it all so seriously. Play with the possibilities.

If you were, in fact, the producer of your life and you had the players and the stage before you, how would the scene play out? Or perhaps this is no longer the movie you want to be in. In this case, call to remembrance a scene where it all plays out according to your truest heart's desires. Then pay attention to what new settings and players come into your life.

DAILY DARE
To Happy Endings

Create the perfect movie that might unfold. The story opens with you standing on a stage. Write the scene as you would like it to play out in your Lifeseeds Journal. Today's dare corresponds to the "Set Your Scene" tool from the Lifeseeds Toolkit.

Lifeseed #50—Flex the Muscle of Your Mind

50

Our minds fixed on a particular way of being in this world, we were frozen in place. We wanted it to be different, but it felt impossible. What was the point? And so we fell into a pattern, day after day, failing to flex the muscle of our minds.

FOCUS TEXT
Flex

Flexibility begins with flex. Before you can exercise your ability to choose the reality you create in your hearts or in your world, you must choose to use the muscle of your mind. Let's boil it down. Mind over matter.

I don't know if you've thought of this before, but if you want to be a body in motion, you might want to master the art of the move. Now, calm down. You don't even have to do an entire revolution.

Flow in your life begins with the flex. Try it. Flex the muscle of your mind. Let your actions follow in its footsteps. If you don't like where you are or where you find yourself to be, get a different routine. Change your mind.

LIFESEED
Flex the Muscle of Your Mind

When we set out to shift our experience by changing our perspective and opening the heart to love, it is essential to harness the power of our minds. Our minds are powerful tools meant to be used in the service of our inspired and fulfilling lives. This cannot happen when we allow thoughts to run the show, leading us first in one direction and then in another.

If we know we want to see movement in our lives, we can invite our minds to be a part of creating meaning, movement, and forward momentum in the direction we determine. If left to its own devices, your mind will likely set its own course. Should this course differ at all from the truest desires of your heart (as it usually does), the result is chaos and confusion. You'll be thrown off course almost before you have begun.

You can change your mind! You can direct it to what matters most to your heart and soul. Use the power of your mind in service of a whole new way of being you and watch how strong you will become.

DAILY DARE
Train Your Brain

An exercise: when your mind begins to wander off on its own course: simply notice and invite it to assist you for the next ten minutes, even if working in the background on creating the experience you most desire. Write about this experiment of flexing the muscle of your mind in your Lifeseeds Journal. Today's dare corresponds to the "Brain Power and the Power to Be" tool from the Lifeseeds Toolkit.

Lifeseed #51—Return to Love

51

The lives we created for ourselves seemed unbearable. Yet, some of us fell in line, vowing to try harder and do better, to follow every rule. Others cast it all aside and turned their backs on everything. In both cases, we left the love that is here and now behind, giving up on gift that is the present.

FOCUS TEXT
Flux

The influx of mind mastery, coupled with a return to your heart's essence — to love — will carry you back into the current. And therein lies the present. It is a cycle of giving and receiving that knows no end. This leads us to the inception of change in you as the exception to the rule.

The rules say you should, you must, and stay within these lines. The rules only became necessary when you forfeited your inner knowing and refused to give way to the turn of the season, to the necessity of change. And then your rules created a false dichotomy between those of you who fell in line, who took your marching orders and fit into society, and those of you who rebelled against the rigidity of what felt false but then found yourselves outside the mainstream.

Many who followed dutifully wake to find themselves far from dreams they thought had died. Too few of you who resisted have persisted. And some who have persisted in following the beat of their own drums have by now wandered so far afield that their voices have been lost or muffled to mere murmur.

Thus, the heartache of humanity.

LIFESEED
Return to Love

When the heart and mind begin to work in partnership, you will experience a new flow in your life. This unrestricted circulation of energy is a gift unlike any other. It is yours when you master your mind and connect to your deepest desires for your life's unfolding journey.

Most people never get this far. They may dream of a better life and wish upon a star. They may also begin to direct their thoughts. It is the rare individual who brings both into harmony and allows the experience of love and joy.

What if you become the exception? The way to come close to lasting change and experiencing the wonder of your life is to return to your natural state. Allow the seasons of your life. Accept and honor the natural process of change. See that *how* you respond to what rules you encounter offers you always a fresh opportunity to choose a new way forward. Allow yourself to choose a way that is aligned with you true nature.

Return to the love alive within you. Begin today to choose a way forward that honors your soul's truth and your life's deepest purpose. Life invites us into a dance of giving and receiving. When you move to the rhythm of love, you are led always onward and back into the gift of flow in your life.

DAILY DARE
Consider Openings
for a Greater Flow of Love

Give yourself this gift. Allow your heart to tell you all it knows. Invite your mind's participation in finding the best way to allow for more love and appreciation in your life. Record what your heart reveals about how you might open to a greater flow of love in your Lifeseeds Journal. Today's dare corresponds to the "Exceptions to the Rule" tool from the Lifeseeds Toolkit.

Lifeseed #52—Open to Full Awareness as You Love What Is

52

We felt jolted and jostled by life's shifts and felt as if we were getting nowhere. Our perspective lost, we failed to see the growth within and gave our attention over to what seemed an erratic sequence of point and counterpoint.

FOCUS TEXT
The Moving Spiral Staircase

Life is always moving us, shifting to the left or right, elevating us or taking us down a few notches. We have to adjust. There are incremental movements we must make as we approach our goal. Sometimes, that means stepping up. Other times, it's just a small adjustment or a pivot to the left or to the right.

When viewed from far away, we can see the beautiful slope of our ascension. You come so close to the next world and barely recognize that you have moved at all. You have been lifted into the realms of angels, but because you find yourself sitting in the same chair or lying beneath your comforter you distrust this. You convince yourself it was just a dream. Or not possible because here you are.

There are two complementary paths we travel as we pass through this life. There is the outer life, the world of weathering the world — its elements, the relationships we form, the work we choose to do, the external challenges and joys. And there is the inner life where, if we are lucky, we begin to see sprouts of growth, new awareness, expanded trust in ourselves, and an ever-widening love for our own humanity. As you love what is, you move toward the unfolding awareness of all that has been.

LIFESEED
Open to Full Awareness as You Love What Is

Things change without warning. Just when we thought we were back on track and making real progress, the curve ball comes flying at us faster than we can blink. This is where our continued attention to our thoughts and emotions, and also our commitment to opening to what they might want to show us, will support us. We can adapt.

The key is to remain fully in the present, choosing in each and every moment the next right step as we adjust to life's "moving spiral staircase." From our viewpoint, it may well appear we have been thrown completely off course. It may be that we cannot always see the whole picture. Life often shifts to meet us at a point of need we have yet to understand. Trust the unfolding.

Wherever you are today, practice presence of mind and bring all the love you hold inside to the situation, mo matter how dire or hopeless it may appear. Love it if only because you are there within it. Respond to change to the best of your ability, and see over time just how far you've come.

DAILY DARE
Giving Thanks for the Unloved Things

Think of three things you do not enjoy about your current life experience. List them on a piece of paper or in your Lifeseeds Journal. Each day, challenge yourself to express one gratitude for the experience. If you can think of nothing good, then simply be present to the difficult situation each day without any move to fix or change it. Today's dare corresponds to the "Presence: Heart, Mind, and Soul" tool from the Lifeseeds Toolkit.

Lifeseed #53—Ease into Life's Curves

53

Life's road was sloping into something new, and at last we were looking forward. Again, we took control and sped on to the long-awaited vista of relief. But we took the curve too fast, forgetting we had all the time we needed.

FOCUS TEXT
Curve Speed

Sometimes we see the long slope of the curve ahead. We know we are transitioning into a stretch of life's highway that leads us gently into something new. We see a little of the way ahead and it looks inviting. The curve seems manageable, something we have waited for, and we think we've got it handled.

You believe you are ready — that this is nothing. And so you hit the gas, in a hurry to get around the bend and see what's on the other side. Take care of the curves. Give yourself the time to ease into them.

There is something to be said for slow and steady. Take the turn too fast and you wipe out, losing more than just a little time.

LIFESEED
Ease into Life's Curves

Watch your speed. Know that making the transition to a whole new way of being is underway and be safe on your journey. You will arrive into the experience fully equipped to maintain this new life when you stay alert and aware around the curves ahead.

There is no need to hurry. Take it easy, giving yourself room on the road from here to there to get used to living in this new way. Adjust as needed, and remember to be patient with the learning process.

When we try to change too much at once or race forward without proper attention to our vehicle (that's your body!), we could be headed for a breakdown. Keep a steady pace, and take care of your mind, body, and spirit, giving them ample time to adjust to the changing landscape of your life.

DAILY DARE
Curve Care Kit

Create your own Curve Care Kit. What would assist your body as you continue to make changes in your life? What would nourish your mind and replenish your spirit? What is your heart whispering it most needs now? Choose one action that would move you closer to fulfilling those needs. Write a statement of commitment to taking this action in your Lifeseeds Journal. Today's dare corresponds to the "Curve Care Commitments" tool from the Lifeseeds Toolkit.

Lifeseed #54—Stay Awake for the Journey

54

Our eye yet fixed on the golden destination of our choice, we changed lanes and pursued our forward progress. In a hurry to get there, we missed all that was here. Who had time for conversation? We never thought to love the ride.

FOCUS TEXT
A Cup of Coffee

You have been conditioned to change lanes quickly, to pursue forward progress onward and upward to the golden gates of some desired final destination. Presumably upon arriving you will know you are there. But in your haste to get where you are going, don't miss the scenery.

Sit down and have a cup of coffee. You never know who you might meet, who might see you smile and let that be enough to carry them through another day. One fine day you might just discover someone smiling back at you. And that might just change the course of your life and put you on the road again to where you were always meant to be.

So, get some coffee. Stay awake for the journey. Love the ride.

LIFESEED

Stay Awake for the Journey, Love Life's Ride

We think we know where we are going, and in many cultures around the world we are in a hurry to get there in record time. We get in such a hurry, we become preoccupied with our lives. We develop tunnel vision, forgetting that part of moving through out lives means enjoying the gift of this present moment.

If you are feeling a push to get there faster, slow down. Take a look around. It is the getting there that is the point, not just that moment of arrival. So pull off the road for a pit stop. There's no time to lose, and there is always time.

Consider something you would enjoy — perhaps something that has nothing at all to do with changing anything. How can you be fully present to receive all that is here for you in this moment along your life's highway?

DAILY DARE

Scenic Overlook Break

Stop at the scenic overlook! Today, we're pulling off the road to enjoy the view. Consider where you were when you started this journey back to life. How has the road unfolded? What have been the key markers so far? What do you see ahead? Take a few moments to enjoy the view, then capture the experience, exploring these questions in your Lifeseeds Journal. Today's dare corresponds to the "Scenic View" tool from the Lifeseeds Toolkit.

Lifeseed #55—Find a Way around Blocks

55

Growling beneath our breath, we pushed on, wearing ourselves down and wearing ourselves out. Stuck in traffic, we cursed again our plight, finding our focus always on the blocks and failing to find a way around. Those blocks became our world.

FOCUS TEXT
Traffic

When something blocks your flow as you move through your life, there are really two choices. One is to grit your teeth and push through at a grinding pace. This will wear you down and wear you out. It will make you old before your time.

The other choice is to pull off the road, take a detour or find a way around, not through. This may delay the gratification of your arrival at the time you deem best. But you will nonetheless arrive and show up in an undeniably better mood than had you stayed, stuck in traffic.

LIFESEED

Find a Way Around Blocks

What's in the way? What is that thing seems like an insurmountable hurdle? Maybe it's a persistent challenging person in your life. Or a problem that keeps coming back.

Let's get creative. Instead of pushing against what seems to be in the way, what if you found a different way? Maybe there's a route that will allow you to move around this "traffic jam" and enjoy your life's ride as you move in the direction of your dreams.

Who wants to be all grumpy, irritated, and constantly sidetracked or at a standstill? Explore new options for the unfolding of your days. See how you might find a way around the blocks.

DAILY DARE

The Blockhead Game

Try the Blockhead Game. Draw a head shape and fill it with rectangles. From each rectangle extend a line with a flower shape on the end of each line. Write one situation that seems to be in your way within each rectangle. Then, consider how you might lessen the negative impact of this reality or find a way around it in your life. If possible, discuss this perceived block that is taking up space within your head with a trusted friend or advisor. Write about the experience in your Lifeseeds Journal. Consider how you can move to the music and find your forward flow, traffic or no traffic, roadblocks or the open highway. Today's dare corresponds to the "Traffic Jam" tool from the Lifeseeds Toolkit.

Lifeseed #56—Begin with Gratitude and Compassion

56

So much had been corrupted. Where was life's purity? No matter how we tried to shed life's dirt and debris, it seemed to cling to us. We sought to cast it off, feeling nothing but disdain, and soon we turned to destruction, spiraling down into dismay and disenchantment with life and with ourselves. We lost sight of the sacred gift, forgetting it was there at all.

FOCUS TEXT
Reclamation

In your world, so much that was pure and nourishing has been corrupted to the degree that it is no longer safe for you. You must learn to separate out those contaminants, some invisible which naturally cling to clean energy. The process of removing what is waste requires discernment, and discernment requires a rigorous examination of all that does not serve the truth.

To reclaim that which was bestowed upon you as a gift of grace, you must begin with gratitude. Give thanks for it. See the perfection within it. Refuse to cast it off as lost, to surrender the gift because it has been contaminated. Instead, choose love and honor. Then, allow that love and honor to lead you to new ideas that restore the gift to its natural state. Think, speak and share thoughts of loving-kindness toward gift and giver.

There is never a need to engage in the cycle of destruction. Transform your thoughts. Turn your anger toward those who have been reckless with the gift into equal action for good. Breathe compassion into the sadness you feel and into your own hearts. Envision the essence and allow what is waste to fall away. Become an advocate for the gift and also for those who have not yet awakened to it and do all you can to support the gift and restore it to its natural state of being.

LIFESEED

Begin with Gratitude and Compassion

With your eyes wide open now, you can see with greater clarity what so quickly clouds your progress. Like fog descending on the highway or pollution being poured out from looming smokestacks, these unwanted distractions can subtly take our attention away from what is most true.

Turn your attention back to you. If you feel your progress has been deterred or stopped altogether due to a cloudy situation from with your heart or from an external source, stop to bring your love and thanks to this opportunity for growth and expansion. Though it may not feel as if it is a gift, trust that, however uncomfortable, this is a situation for your betterment.

Ask for help if needed. Invite your heart, mind, and spirit to work together to find your way through to a clear path forward. Stop for awhile and wait for the clearing.

Should you feel attacked at any point along the way, turn your anger into acts of kindness toward yourself and wherever possible toward the one whose actions have caused you harm. Protect the treasure of your heart and begin again at a pace that feels best.

DAILY DARE

Look for a Break in the Clouds

Do you ever feel that clouds have descended and you cannot see your way forward? Become aware of them, and turn your eyes back to the treasure in your heart. Trust you will be led, and look for a break in the clouds. Walk forward with confidence, grateful for each and every step. In your Lifeseeds Journal, write one area of your life in which you may feel lost or off track. Explore one way you will choose to take a next step, trusting the road to rise up to meet you on your way. Today's dare corresponds to the "The Clearing" tool from the Lifeseeds Toolkit.

Lifeseed #57—Give Thanks for All that Nourishes

57

Every day, life dragged on, an ordinary drudgery. We tired of the daily bread, which seemed a meager gift for all our hard work. Around and around we went, oblivious to the beauty and the blessing.

FOCUS TEXT
Breaking Bread

But here, you say, you have to eat. There are always hungry mouths to feed, and it is a nuisance. You tire of the mundane and the profane. And so you go through the day muttering complaint after complaint against the day and all that fills it. You wholly miss the holy, and that there is extravagance hidden there within your ordinary. Extraordinary. And altogether unnecessary.

When you break the bread, remember it is a gift. Your money may have purchased this particular loaf, but you have not invented bread or manifested it from thin air. Perhaps such a miracle might occur but not so long as you pat yourself on the back and recite to yourself that you have worked hard and this is all that you have. And tomorrow you will get up and repeat the cycle. Break the chain of pride locked so tight around your hearts and minds that you have cut yourself off from the remembrance of the bread of life broken for all of you, the manna that nourishes your body and spirit, and the grace of those gathered round your table.

Drink the new wine, and, please, get yourselves some new wineskins. There's really no cause for drivel, complaint, and repetition in the presence of mystery made manifest. Get it together. Receive a bounty of blessing. Give thanks for the fancy of the feast and the grace of the meager meal.

LIFESEED
Give Thanks for All That Nourishes

The practical side of life can become an annoyance when we fail to bring our whole hearts to this aspect of our lives. Notice your complaints. Do not judge yourself for having fallen into this trap. Rather, simply turn toward thanksgiving.

Be thankful for the food you have to eat, for the place you have to sleep, even if it is not what you had imagined for your life. Come to these things that seem unimpressive and ordinary. View them with new appreciation. Be grateful for small and simple gifts that nourish and enrich your life.

Let all you have become be a bounty of blessing. Consider the extraordinary ways it enriches your whole experience. See who is present in your life and celebrate their presence.

DAILY DARE
Fifty Ways

In your Lifeseeds Journal, list fifty ways you have all you need in your life as it is now. The next time you find yourself resorting to complaint about your circumstances, read your list and give thanks for all that nourishes. Today's dare corresponds to the "Fifty Fifty" tool from the Lifeseeds Toolkit.

Lifeseed #58—Get in the Story

58

Determined to make something of our lives,

we sought to rise above life. We studied it from afar, all the while closing our hearts, pretending to be impervious to its sweeping grace. We counted our coins or made precise notes. We offered pleasantries from a distance, having decided it was the only way.

FOCUS TEXT

Get in the Story

Are you comfortable just watching all of life unfold from a good vantage point? Have you scurried up a tree? Do you like to live above the fray? Look out! The big story will rush to fill the smallest hearts. You are never beyond the reach of love. Never.

What goes up must come down. Those who believe they've got one up on life are never as happy as they appear. Neither are they as alone as they may feel. It does not matter who has given up on you. It does not matter that you have given up on yourself. It only matters that you come down from your perch and get in the story.

Because you *are* the story.

LIFESEED
Get in the Story

If you want to live fully, you've go to get in the game. You can't stay on the sidelines and know what it is to catch the perfect pass or help the team move the chains down the field. You will never feel the joy of rounding the bases toward home or hear the cheers ring out for you if you simply sit it out.

This life is yours, and love will make its way to you. If you are only afraid of a broken heart or a losing game, remember life is on your side and that love will find a way.

Step into your life and allow your story to unfold. It will surprise you, and you will soon feel the joy of being on the way. In time, you will know what it is to be celebrated for who you are, beginning with your celebration of you.

DAILY DARE
The View from the Stands

It's time for a report from the sidelines of your life. Are you afraid of your life's journey? On one side of a page, or in your Lifeseeds Journal, record all the things that could potentially happen, good and bad. Then, on the other side of the page, list all the things you can never experience from the stands, just outside the action that is as unpredictable as it is exciting. Today's dare corresponds to the "View from the Stands" tool from the Lifeseeds Toolkit.

Lifeseed #59—Find Favor, Not Fault

59

One day, we noticed it — the tiny crack that had widened. Despite our efforts to move through life unscathed, we fell into its inescapable wound. We could not comprehend how, though we furiously sought to fill up our lives with all they seemed to lack, still there was this ache, like a hole within our hearts.

FOCUS TEXT
Fault Lines

Are you experiencing divisions in your relationships at home or at work? Are there deep gaps in your fulfillment? Are you always sinking lower into the valley of sadness? Are your voices echoing like doves crying out and clashing against the canyon walls before fading into frosted silence? Is there friction?

Go back in time and you're likely to find fault lines. The moment you blamed the other a tiny crack in the foundation was formed. Over time, the blame and the shame, the contempt and the endless criticism eroded the very foundation of your relationship, wearing down the solid rock. And you became two plates, made of the same stuff but pulled in opposite directions.

The stress became too much and what you thought would surely stand the test of time crumbled before your eyes. Stop looking for someone else to make up for what you lack. Take responsibility for every word and every action. Surrender your desperate search to fill the holes in your life and all you think is missing from you.

Try something new. Start finding favor. Start filling in the cracks in the foundation with love. Plant flowers of faith, living into another Spring.

LIFESEED
Find Favor, Not Fault

Do you experience loneliness, anger, or sadness in your relationships with others? The invitation to the dance of your life today is to consider where you may have cast blame toward an individual or a group of people you saw as responsible for a less-than-desirable experience.

Or perhaps you compared yourself to that one and assessed yourself as not measuring up. Maybe you buried the shame you felt at having made a choice that was not honoring of yourself or the other person. Is it possible you had hoped this other person could give you something you thought you did not have?

In ever day encounters, practice finding favor and planting the seeds of fruitful relationships that will stand the test of time. Bring joy to you and to the other person where it is possible to do so, and look for goodness.

DAILY DARE
Flowers of Faith

Consider a particular relationship in your life. How can you plant flowers of faith and find favor in this relationship? Explore this in detail in your Lifeseeds Journal today. Today's dare corresponds to the "Flowers of Faith" tool from the Lifeseeds Toolkit.

Lifeseed #60—Cultivate Cooperation

60

We decided things. We drew our own conclusions about this life and proved out our theories. In the end, we were as alone as ever, having separated ourselves from life and those with whom we share the journey.

FOCUS TEXT
Cooperation

Some of you have come to the altogether scientific conclusion that God is not active in your world. You don't see it because you have chosen not to believe it. You formed a hypothesis and set out to prove yourself correct. And, surprise, you did!

When you look at all the evidence gathered by all of those looking at the question, the fact of the matter appears in the form of energy, elusive but no less powerful a conclusion. Work together, and you will see.

LIFESEED
Cultivate Cooperation

Believe, and you will see. What have you chosen to believe? Inevitably we are drawn to evidence to support the beliefs we choose. In light of this reality, we must examine the hypothesis with which we begin our investigation and exploration of life. What would you most like to be the truth of your experience? What kind of world do you hope to live in?

When we choose community and a system of coordination and cooperation that begins with honor and respect for our own contribution and for that of all others as equally essential to the full flowering of life, we experience the gift of harmony. It is far easier to shut ourselves off from others and even to write off the existence of God or hope or love.

Choose a new way of being present to possibility. Open to life, and consider its nature anew.

DAILY DARE
Seven Beginning Words

Consider your quality of life. List seven ways you have seen your life. Note all the signs that what you have believed is true. Now, choose seven new words and collect new evidence as you choose a whole new way of being who you are. Make note of the new things you are looking for in your life in your Lifeseeds Journal. Today's dare corresponds to the "Seven First Words" tool from the Lifeseeds Toolkit.

Lifeseed #61—See Truth When It Surprises You

61

There came the startling present of the truth, shaking all our presuppositions about who we were and why we had come. Yet, we were afraid of what such a great love revealed would mean, and so we set about reordering worlds if only to salvage all we thought left to save.

FOCUS TEXT
Surprise!

A moment will come that will appear, for better or worse, to have been destined. It will seem as if, for all your life, you had been being drawn toward this single moment when you come face to face with a startling truth that changes you. Perhaps the truth is a something. Perhaps it is someone — your beloved or your betrayer.

This moment of truth revealed is inevitable, but the element of surprise is not lost. Ultimately, it's all up to you. Will you recognize the truth or scramble to reorder entire worlds if only to protect the sanctity of the illusion you had created for yourself?

LIFESEED
See Truth When It Surprises You

Has life ever revealed a surprising truth to you? What was your response?

Such an encounter can touch us at our core. We may feel exposed and experience a whole host of thoughts and feelings. Many of us panic and rush to stem the tide of emotions we do not understand.

It can be tempting to deny the truth that rises up in such moments. In the past we may have gone to great lengths to shield our eyes and turn our hearts away. To do otherwise was simply too terrifying at the time. Or seemed to require too much of us.

There comes a time when we must choose to be steadfast and true to our own souls above all else that may seem "right" and worthy of our time and attention. This does not mean we make flippant choices or cause pain to others as we move to embrace our own truth. Rather, we have always the opportunity to be grateful for new levels of awareness and then trust life to present a way that allows for both soul integrity and respect and loving-kindness for all life.

DAILY DARE
The Moment of Truth

What has been a moment of truth for you? What did you choose? How will you recognize such a moment when it presents itself to you in your life? How will you greet the "surprise" that leads you to a whole new experience of your life? Explore this further in your Lifeseeds Journal. Today's dare corresponds to the "Moment of Truth" tool from the Lifeseeds Toolkit.

Lifeseed #62—Treasure the Dance of Life

62

So it is that life presents the gift of the present, and it often comes packaged in surprise. We may push it away or think it a trick, wait for a better day, or tear into it and then just as quickly cast it aside. We may see the truth that it is gift and still persist in making a case against it, because it disrupts our plans.

FOCUS TEXT
Open the Present, Already!

It's been sitting right there, forever, hidden in plain sight. Will you choose to receive the full realization of what you have always known? Will you reject it outright? Or will you sit there admiring the bow and the wrapping as if that is the whole of the gift?

Some of you question why the gift should be there, thinking it must be some kind of mistake. Some have been known to grab the present, tear into it with a ferocious spirit and then just as quickly cast it aside.

The surprising truth is this: when that moment of now arrives you are either ready or you are not. Surprisingly, it's all up to you. Do you cycle through the lessons, one by one, and move on swiftly to the next?

Or do you lock horns with the devil in the detail and do battle to the death? Have you considered what is sacrificed when you insist on being right, deconstructing the truth revealed piece by piece? You see the result before you: tattered pieces. You forget this is merely a reflection of what you have done to your own heart and soul.

How invested are you in your choice? How long do you want to take to learn to dance with life? There's no real hurry. Take your time to decide what kind of life you want. Or get up from your seat and dance with destiny.

LIFESEED
Treasure the Dance of Life

We're forever playing the game of When / Then and the game of How / Now. The When / Then game goes like this: we say, "I will be happy when…" or "Once that happens then I can finally…". We delay saying yes to the dance of our lives and hinge our happiness on the occurrence of some future event.

The How / Now game is a go-to pattern and program for many of us. Imagine the sound of a child whining. "How can I possibly enjoy this experience now that…," you ask. After this opening, we typically list all the reasons, some logical and some dressed up in what appears to be genuine concern for others. We may list even more reasons to explain why the timing is just not right yet. Again, we put off what life has brought before us as gift.

The alternative to these approaches is to treasure every moment, no matter the degree of preparation or perfection we feel within it. We can choose to believe that we can enter into the moment, regardless of what is happening, with our whole hearts, knowing we are complete and can find contentment and love within ourselves.

How are you responding to life's gift today? Are you opening the present? Have you forgotten that it is waiting for you within?

DAILY DARE
What Will You Do with this Day Gift?

Notice in which of these ways you are most prone to act: Do you reject the gift? Do you see it but simply admire the pretty packaging, not daring to open it for fear of what it might require of you? Do you think it a trick? Do you tear into the gift of the day and then discard it? Ready or not, here life is. Do you want to dance? Or will you turn your back again? Consider these questions in your Lifeseeds Journal. Today's dare corresponds to the "Presenting the Present" tool from the Lifeseeds Toolkit.

Lifeseed #63—Let Go of a Need for Compensation

63

We demand our just reward, having sacrificed so much. Having learned to compensate for what we thought we had to set aside, we fled from the very truth that might have set us free. We settle, bargain, beg, or steal. We meet this gracious life with sarcasm, cynicism, and a boiling contempt beneath the placid smile and wait for a moment that never comes.

FOCUS TEXT
Compensation

Everybody wants his due — some reward for having survived the fray and having made it through another day. We learn this well as little children who have arrived in a world, or a family that is our world, where we are under-appreciated or not even seen for who we truly are.

We shrink. We set our true value aside in order to survive the harrowing passages of growing up. Knowing this to be a raw deal, we learn to compensate.

So, if we came here laughing and filled with light but found ourselves trapped in an environment where free expression was simply not permitted, we may have felt squelched, silenced, shut down, or swallowed up by the serious. Maybe you were bewildered for having come to such a place as this. In such a case, one might become skilled at the art of snarkiness and sarcasm. We become the cynic.

Or we put on the straight face like a straight jacket and perfect our act to such a degree that we take the show on the road. This is, after all, our just reward. This is the lie we tell ourselves. Such compensation is nothing of the sort. It robs us blind. And yet, if we are lucky, this leads us back to the stage. There, at first, we simply play out the same drama, night after night. But this very stage can become the place where we rediscover our joy and wonder. One day, perhaps, we laugh again.

LIFESEED
Let Go of a Need for Compensation

You may think you've paid your dues. It's time life paid you back. This is what's really running through our minds sometimes. The desire for recognition and reward is a shared one.

When we find ourselves feeling left out and cast aside, we can choose to turn our love toward that deep longing to receive. We can give the gift of presence to our souls. Let your heart ache for the ways you have not been there for yourself. Be present to the pain without demanding recompense.

Maybe at some earlier time in your life you could not find the capacity to be present. The pain simply felt too immense. So instead you may have covered it with addiction or busyness. Or maybe you simply surrendered to the way it seemed to work in your family or in the world.

Did you ever take the time to grieve this loss? Or did you become bitter and cynical, your heart hardened to life's injury? Did you perhaps leave that most important part of you behind in your desire to fit in and make it all okay?

If anywhere in your life you have been trading authenticity for some short-lived feeling of relief, reconsider this pattern. See the play you acted in and the part you have played in trading truth for something temporary. Learn to laugh, and love yourself again.

DAILY DARE
Go Ahead, Make a Cheat Sheet

Create a "cheat sheet" that lists the ways you have felt "cheated" by life. Then, in your Lifeseeds Journal, write about a decision you made about who you were or conclusions you drew about life as a result of this experience. Finally, listen to what your heart and soul would tell you about a new decision that will lead you to a reclamation of joy. Today's dare corresponds to the "Cheat Sheet / Heart Part" tool from the Lifeseeds Toolkit.

Lifeseed #64—Listen to Your Body

64

We deny ourselves, possibly cutting ourselves off from the experience of being in human form. We pretend not to notice the body's dialogue and treat it with disregard. Distanced, we further divide the gift of this life.

FOCUS TEXT
Let Me Hear Your Body Talk

We are living in a material world where matter matters. Your body gets a vote, so why do you push it away and subjugate it and say it doesn't matter? It matters. It is matter.

You are neither separate from your body nor defined by it. You are not your body, but you are not meant to simply dwell in your body. You are meant to dance with it as a partner, to marvel at the way it moves you in this world.

Listen to your body. What does it want to tell you? What ideas does it long to express? How does it want to get you where you want to go? What can you learn from it? How might you honor it, nourish it, and appreciate the very gift of it?

LIFESEED
Listen to Your Body

Many of us have trouble with our bodies. They feel old and worn down. Worn out by life, we can become numb to our physical experience. We make it less important than all the other priorities in our life.

Do you see your body as separate from the whole of you? Or do you see your body as the whole of you? Both create barriers to the full experience of being human. Practice reconnection to your body. Bring your attention to your physical shape and form. Treat your body as if it matters, and remind yourself that it is, by definition, matter.

One way to do this is to open a conversation with your body. What does your body want to tell you? What can it show you? What is it dying for you to know? What is its greatest joy in living this life with you?

DAILY DARE
Body Talk

Try a little "body talk." In your Lifeseeds Journal, explore how you really feel about your body. Are you in synch with it or disconnected? Do you feel awkward about particular parts of your physical experience? Do certain parts of your body bring up fear or anger, grief or sadness? Listen to what you body is saying and be present to that. Today's dare corresponds to the "Body Flower Power" tool from the Lifeseeds Toolkit.

Lifeseed #65—Know Where You Belong

65

We feel the stir of a wild desire or hear the beating of a different drum. Yet, who are we to dare to be anyone special? We doubt the truth that rises up and wear the labels this world would put upon us all too willingly. We drone louder, hoping to drown out all the noise, caught up in the story of who we are meant to be, face to face with choice and sovereignty.

FOCUS TEXT

Out of the Hive and into the Cuckoo's Nest

Busy bees are all abuzz about the one that got away. And should that one revolutionary bee miss the sweet honey and come back to the clan, he's sure to be stung.

The worker bee who dares to abandon his assigned post or fails to serve his queen gets labeled crazy. The world fills up with the noise of clucking that follows him, saying louder and louder that he belongs in the cuckoo's nest.

But only you know where you belong. If you are a bee, be a bee. But not all bees are meant to drone on endlessly. There is the life sweeter than honey. Sometimes to get it, you have to leave the hive.

LIFESEED
Know Where You Belong

The cuckoo bird is a stunningly original bird with odd looks. With a spike hairstyle reminiscent of the '80s and a wide-eyed stare, it flaunts its long, distinguished-looking tail that becomes a rudder as the bird takes flight.

It's a difficult thing in this world to stand out or to go your own way. If you dare to do it, there will undoubtedly be clucking all about. Some will call you crazy. Some will shun you from communities rooted in conformity or ordered hierarchies that demand you stay put where the acting regent deems your place to be.

There comes a point in life where we have to learn to trust ourselves more than all of those voices combined. What do you know about yourself that you may have been afraid to say out loud, much less act upon? Within you, you have all you need to fly to the places where you are free to live authentically and free from the arbitrary constraints others would place upon you.

Trust that. Be who you and only you can be, buzz or no buzz.

DAILY DARE
The Sweet Life

What is your sweet life? Imagine you are free to be exactly who you are designed to be. Where would you fly and why? Write a description of a life where you are contributing your gifts, happy and belonging wholly to yourself and to this life. Write a vision of you living this life, in present tense, in your Lifeseeds Journal. Today's dare corresponds to the "My Bee Cause" tool from the Lifeseeds Toolkit.

Lifeseed #66—Love Yourself First

66

Someone makes a pronouncement and places on our lives a mantle of shame. We begin to believe we are flawed, forever burdened by what was once bestowed as gift. We try to set our lives aright, fit into society. We think we have been eaten alive, reduced to a shattered offering. We turn away from loving this life.

FOCUS TEXT
Aphids and Aphrodite

Zeus thought the other gods would be threatened by the beauty of Aphrodite. He surmised that they would be undone by jealousy. And so she was shuttled off into a loveless marriage.

Punished for who she was, Aphrodite felt such pain around this that she turned to others and wound up hurting all the more. Those who shove others into shadow are no more than hungry aphids that destroy the cultivated beauty of plants. When your beautiful spirit begins to wither, love yourself. Go within. Love yourself first; then, make wise choices aligned with loving and valuing you. Aphrodite, when her gifts were thought to shine too brightly, began to believe the lie. She created the only way she knew to keep some part of her soul alive. She compensated for the belief she was too beautiful and would provoke jealousy. She fulfilled it.

No matter what aphids eat you alive, your essence cannot be taken from you. Know that those parts of you that show up to fill the void arise to be your champions and protectors. Thank them for coming. Love them. Love the you they came to love. Forgive yourself for any mis-takes that arose because who you were was not seen and valued by others — or by you yourself.

LIFESEED
Love Yourself First

You will meet people during your life's journey who are convinced that they know best what you need. They may steer you toward certain actions and choices, often with the best of intentions. If you choose to listen first to them over your own inner guidance — or should you love that one more than you love yourself, you may walk down a path that leads to pain.

The aphid is a mere one to ten millimeters in length. If you don't have perfect eye site, you are liable to miss it entirely. Barely visible, this pervasive species nevertheless does millions of dollars in damage to crops and other plant life each year. The aphids weaken and destroy plant life, and they multiply sometimes producing as many as six generations within a single year of life.

Like the aphids that devour plants, there will always be fellow travelers on our human journey who would, knowingly or unknowingly, do damage to our souls and sap our energy for life. This is why in life it is critical to love ourselves first and to choose for ourselves, making decisions informed first by what we know of ourselves. It is most tempting to listen first to those we look up to and admire or to adopt their beliefs as our own.

Whatever your choices have been until now and whatever arises in the wake of your own pain at having compromised the truth you carry within, choose today a path of forgiveness and love for others and, most of all, for yourself.

DAILY DARE
Transforming Regret

Consider choices you have made that you may have come to regret. Write these down on a page. Then use paints or crayons to transform these choices into a beautiful picture. Allow the creation process to be an act of self-love and self-forgiveness. Keep this picture in a special place, perhaps in your Lifeseeds Journal, to remind you of your beauty. Today's dare corresponds to the "The Picture of Forgiveness" tool from the Lifeseeds Toolkit.

Lifeseed #67—Notice How You Are Moving through Life

67

We move through life, just trying to avoid the bumps and bruises and miss the next opportunity window of the now. We are constantly looking around, comparing who we are to what we see. We tell ourselves a story about how we measure up. Whether we conform or go against the grain, we run from the fullness of who we are.

FOCUS TEXT
Matriculation

Here's the deal: when you sign up for school, you're gonna go to class. Learning will happen. It's unlikely that you will ace every life test and soar through unscathed.

But when you dare to show up day after day after day and do the work, it's really not about the grades. The bells and attendance and homework grades are simply the trappings of school. The real deal is the conversation in the classroom, and that includes the conversation you're having with you about you in addition to the discussion of facts and figures pertinent to your reality.

Do you go through life comparing yourself to others? Do you make a conscious or subconscious choice to subjugate who you are and conform? Do you settle for just getting by? Do you do your work at the last possible moment? Do you measure yourself merely by a letter on a report card or do you dare to get involved in the real work happening all around you?

It's about making it through to the day you toss the cap up in the air without succumbing to the expectation of perfection and without dropping out. It's about learning to work in groups with difficult people. It's about stretching the bounds of what you know. It's about coming back to balance, so that you can say yes with authority to the next opportunity. It's about having compassion for yourself. Most of all, it's about finding the courage to do your best and to be yourself.

LIFESEED
Notice How You Are Moving through Life

Life comes with certain mandatory experiences. Interacting with other people, learning to care for our bodies, and getting a handle on the shared agreements of our society or culture are three must-do examples. It can be easy to feel pressured to be perfect.

Many of us feel quite defeated when we realize we fall far short of perfect. Or we might become numb to the routine and lose touch with the true purpose of our lives — the actual experience of living. Check in with your whole self and your soul self.

What have you been telling yourself about your life? How do you show up for you and for life? Or do you? Have you been taking the easy way out and simply moving from one day to the next without taking the time to fully feel and appreciate all that is unfolding?

Do you get along with the crowd? Or do you find a way out of the experiences and encounters that scare you. Do you avoid life or do you move into its current? Consider what could make this life really fun for you. How can you open up and learn something new today?

DAILY DARE
The Be Leaf Exercise

Today, take part in what I call the "Belief / Be Leaf" exercise. Think about the story you have told yourself about who you are and what life is. Summarize a core belief in a sentence or two. Now, imagine the way you want to feel about yourself as you move through your life. In your Lifeseeds Journal, write an "I Am" statement to represent the experience you wish to have in the shape of a leaf. Look at your Be-Leaf as you begin your day each morning to instill more of this feeling in the experience of each new day and watch your belief transform into a growing thing. Today's dare corresponds to the "Belief / Be Leaf" tool from the Lifeseeds Toolkit.

Lifeseed #68—Balance Work, Play, and Rest

68

In our fury to keep up with work, whether to prove ourselves to ourselves or to others, and in our love of fun and play, we sometimes forget to rest. We shortchange both our contribution to the world and the gift of presence to ourselves when we fail to stop and replenish our bodies, minds, and spirits.

FOCUS TEXT
Cycles of Work and Play

Work. Play. Sleep. Rinse and repeat. It's really not that complicated.

Work is contribution. When you share your gifts and talents, you value the world and those who share it with you. You give back. Work is our gift to the world. Play is our gift to ourselves and to one another.

Rest is required for both. Sometimes, it's important to play at work and work at play. Both are enhanced when you mix in a little rest. Remember nap time? Siesta makes possible the fiesta of life and work. So, take a break.

LIFESEED
Balance Work, Play, and Rest

Work, play, and rest are equally important to a balanced life. Each affects the quality of the other. We could learn a lot by going back to childhood days. Sleep gave us energy for play. Play made it easier to get through whatever "work" we may have been assigned. If we were lucky, helping out brought a measure of meaning to our lives.

Work and play are about activity. We are applying our energy and creativity to life when we engage in these activities. We feel more alive as we show up fully and contribute in ways that bring joy to our individual lives. Often, the places we apply our energy also contribute something to our community or to the whole of the human experience.

But all that activity depends on a time of restfulness. Without attending to cycles of rest, our lives will remain imbalanced, resulting in decreased satisfaction and impeding our life's full flow. When work, play, and rest are out of balance, we shortchange the vision for our life and delay or even impede our ability to bring that vision to life through vibrant, integrated, and soul-inspired offerings now.

DAILY DARE
LIFE Tri-Cycle Evaluation

The LIFE Tri-Cycle Evaluation invites you to examine the full-circle systems of work, play, and rest that enable us to live most fully. Explore these three areas in your Lifeseeds Journal. Questions to consider: Are you balancing your gifts to yourself through play, your gifts to the world through work and meaningful contribution? Do you get enough rest? Adjust your schedule as you are able and find creative ways to bring balance to your life. Today's dare corresponds to the "LIFE Tri-Cycle Evaluation" tool from the Lifeseeds Toolkit.

Lifeseed #69—Stand in the Stream of Your Life

69

We stand apart and judge the world as insufficient to our need. We ask if this is all there is, having already cut ourselves off from all that is seeking us. Still, we are avoiding the current of our lives. With one foot in and one foot out, we are straddling two worlds and two ways of being. We cannot know who we might be, holding such a stance.

FOCUS TEXT
Seeking Something

Change what you're looking for and see what you find. If nobody's ever there for you, be there for somebody and watch what happens. If there's never enough, look for all the places where there is more than enough. If you can't seem to get a break, stop looking for one and walk in the way until you see an opening. Seek and you will find.

So often, you stand alone on a far-off horizon and judge the world for being unsatisfactory. You're looking for something more, but you have separated yourself from the life you seek. Stand in the stream and feel the flow. Only then can you gain the perspective required to carry you through. Only the experience of being immersed in life gives you the qualification to assess its give and take.

LIFESEED
Stand in the Stream of Your Life

Complaining is a habit we fall into if we are not paying close attention to the hours and moments and days of our lives. It is a habit most often fueled by our inner awareness that we are not fully engaged in the living of our own life. To avoid seeing this, we find creative ways to justify our non-participation. We may find fault with others and life itself. Or we may simply throw up our hands and proclaim it is too hard.

If you have formed a conclusion about life that is essentially keeping you stuck, playfully choose to turn it on its head. Prove to yourself that even if this statement were true, you can take action and step into or give the thing you think will never come to you.

Dare to look for the opposite. Essentially, become willing to see life differently and show up in a way that demonstrates something entirely new or different than all you may have once believed.

Dare to step into life's current and seek what you truly most want to find as you stand in the center and become that thing. It's time now to remember what it really feels like to become one with life. No more standing on the shore and saying it's all hopeless and you will never belong to it. Come on in. The water's fine, and your life is waiting to meet you when you step into a whole new way of freeing yourself from old ways you have outgrown.

DAILY DARE
Give the Gift You Are Wishing For

Make a list of desired life experiences in your Lifeseeds Journal today. What do you most wish to see or experience? How can you give this thing to another? Commit to choosing one thing you would like to feel or experience and offering that as a gift to another person. Be open to all the ways this experience reveals itself as a gift in your life. Today's dare corresponds to the "Three Wishes, Three Gifts" tool from the Lifeseeds Toolkit.

Lifeseed #70—Carry Your Truth in Grace

70

We made our own way, seeking to shield ourselves from the pain of relationship. Some of us thought it all an accident and learned to doubt what our soul's longed to share. Others raised their voice to proclaim the truth, seeking converts and confession. Unbending, we fought against the life that would set us free.

FOCUS TEXT
The Context of Community

It is when we gather together, we begin to see what's possible. We first understand what we do want and what we don't want in light of the contrasting experiences we discover as we connect and converse with others on the way. In relationship to one another, we seek and, inevitably, we find ourselves again — whether through joy or disappointment, faithfulness or abandonment, bliss or brokenness.

We remember, if only in bits and pieces and fits and starts, that we are not here by accident. We are our teachers, and the lesson is this: we have come for this very purpose. We have come to reawaken fully to the truth that we are the creators, the sovereign rulers and intrepid explorers of our own lives, adventurers in this world we spin with for a time.

In family and friendship we find flickers of the truth. Whether we are loved deeply and held closely or cast out to fend for ourselves, in the substrate of every cell we know whether such an experience is resonant with the one truth or a distortion of it. We feel such things every day but only discover truth fully when we give up the damned determination to make our own way, as if we were the only ones who ever had a once upon a time.

So come together. Observe. Know what you already know. Allow it to be. Give others the grace to see what is for themselves. Deep truths cannot be hawked like silver watches from where the sidewalks meet. Carry your truth in grace. Hold the space for them even as you direct your own life in the way the river flows.

LIFESEED
Carry Your Truth in Grace

Another reason to get off the sidelines and participate in the full flowering of your life is that connections with others offer us insights into our lives, providing a much clearer understanding of our own gifts, dreams, and perspectives. Relationships can serve as a mirror, reconnecting us to all that matters most in us.

When we are around each other, it is easier to see the uniqueness of who we are. It is also more difficult to believe the lie we tell ourselves: that we have nothing to offer. You are the champion of your life. You are the explorer, the dreamer, the actor on the stage. We feel this in flashes when we are around one another. And then, all too often, we shrink back.

Where can you come together with others and begin to listen to your own truth? Are you present to what is held within your heart? How might you practice "carrying your own truth in grace" as you move out into the world and into the dance of your one beautiful, magnificent, extraordinary life?

DAILY DARE
Connections to Community

Create a Community Connection Appreciation Tracker. As you practice connecting with other in various groups and communities, keep a log of all the ways you receive from such experiences. Also track your growing awareness of truths you hold within and particular gifts along your life's unfolding journey in your Lifeseeds Journal. Today's dare corresponds to the "Community Appreciation Log" tool from the Lifeseeds Toolkit.

Lifeseed #71—Listen for the Song of Your Soul

71

There came a stillness after the storm. We walked alone and heard the distant melody and the sound of a rushing river deep within. We stood on the edge of our lives, met in the moment of choice.

FOCUS TEXT
The Music of Solitude

In the stillness, a melody rises from within. When you walk alone, whether by choice or by losses too vast to measure, you find a way both to find and to follow the music. Alone, there can be no mistaking the sound of truth for a lost strand of conversation or background noise. One can only believe she is crazy for so long.

Listen to your soul when life leaves you on your own. There are the keys waiting to be played. There you will find your song.

Once, before life sprang up around a fertile crescent lush and green, a river ran through it. Here we stand at the moment of discovery. First, we must see the river and become it. One with its essence, we will find our flow and birth worlds of wonder. If we choose.

LIFESEED
Listen For the Song of Your Soul

Some of us find ourselves with what seems to be a sort of forced solitude. For many reasons, we may not have access at some times in our lives to loving communities or groups of friends and family who are able to walk with us on our journeys. This is a source of genuine sadness at times.

These times when we walk alone offer a unique opportunity to listen again to the song within our hearts and to know what is most true to us. You may discover something new about who you are. As you see more clearly than ever that love flows through you, choose deliberately to align your life with that river. It will lead you through your life and into experiences of wonder you have not yet dared to imagine.

DAILY DARE
The Keys of Your Life's Song

Think about the qualities that make you uniquely you. Are you patient and kind, bold and colorful, compassionate or strong? Listen to the song within and consider all that makes you who you are. Be curious. Draw keys to your life song on a page in your Lifeseeds Journal, making note of the major tones in your life's song. Today's dare corresponds to the "Keys to Life" tool from the Lifeseeds Toolkit.

{3}

Life Transformation
for Radiant Expansion

Embrace a New Vision for the Nexus of Change
A Whole New Way of Freeing Yourself

Introduction to the Life Transformation Journey

The Life Transformation Journey focuses on radiant expansion to embrace a new vision for the nexus of change in our life. We are embracing a whole new way of freeing ourselves and remembering we are love. Think of the pathways or seeds for life below as invitations to further explore the territory of your soul and embrace a new vision for the nexus of change in your life. In this third journey, we are remembering, **I AM LOVE**.

About Life Transformation Lifeseeds

Think of the momentum action pathways (MAPs) that follow as your living map as you further explore the territory of your soul and embrace a new vision for the nexus of change. The pathways opened up by the seeds for life below correspond to the passages found in the third movement of *Cultivating Essence from the Matrix of Soul* and are explored in the book, *Embracing a New Vision*.

Seeds for Life from the Life Transformation Soul Journey

LIFE TRANSFORMATION LIFESEEDS

72. MOVE TO THE MUSIC OF THE QUESTIONS
73. SEE YOURSELF AS A CYCLE OF CHANGE
74. ENGAGE IN VALUE REDEFINITION
75. STAND IN SACRED TIME
76. BREATHE IN PROMISE REVEALED
77. SEE THE INTRICATE BEAUTY OF LIFE UNFOLDING
78. KNOW THAT BEAUTY BEGINS WITHIN
79. FIND WHAT FEELS GOOD
80. CHOOSE AND CHOOSE AGAIN
81. FIND THE EXPERIENCE THAT BRINGS OUT YOUR BEST
82. CULTIVATE PERSPECTIVE AND BALANCE
83. CONSIDER FORM AND FUNCTION
84. EMBRACE CHANGE
85. CELEBRATE CHOICE AND CREATIVE CONTRIBUTION
86. HOLD FAST TO THE TRUTH OF WHO YOU ARE
87. UNBIND YOURSELF AND FLY FREE
88. RISK THE JOURNEY
89. RETAIN YOUR SENSE OF PLAY AND ADVENTURE
90. KNOW THE END IS THE BEGINNING

Lifeseed #72—Move to the Music of the Questions

72

Scouring the distant horizon and looking down at our feet, still we have searched high and low for the answer. We waited for a revelation from the skies — some sign that now was the time. Uncomfortable with a swirl of questions and uncertainty, we hesitated, shielding ourselves from all we did not yet comprehend, and missing the keys to life within.

FOCUS TEXT
Stop Waiting for the Answer

Stop waiting for the answer. Stop looking for the way. Start moving to the music of the questions. Start walking. Allow your soul to dance. Open your eyes to skies dappled with possibility and infuse each day with a celebration of choice. Raise yourself. Elevate your life. Grow your soul.

Stop waiting to be lifted by the hand of heaven. Reframe the very concept of change by seeing it as not only constant but also the predictable opportunity for some new beginning inside of every perceived ending.

Know one another. Allow yourself to be vulnerable. Dare to find yourselves there in the questions emerging from your life.

LIFESEED
Move To the Music of the Questions

Are you waiting for life to make sense? Have you been waiting for a break — your chance to see some opening in what seems a bleak, no-way-out situation? Did you forget all the choices that are still yours to make?

In whatever situation you find yourself, you may choose to direct your attention within. There, in time, you will find the keys to a whole new way of freeing yourself that is not dependent upon where you are or how things are going in your life.

Vulnerability scares the life out of us. We aren't very good, most of us, at just being present to questions without trying to force an answer. When we can remain present and make choices that reorient us in the direction of joy and peace, we do our part, so that the waters that threaten to consume us may one day part or we may be guided safely through them.

DAILY DARE
Your Question Mark

Today, dance with the questions. Make a list of all the questions for which you would like answers. Include every question that arises, no matter how much space you fill. As you write shape the questions into a form, perhaps an oversized question mark, a flower, or a dancer. In your Lifeseeds Journal, create a symbol, doodle, or drawing to remind you to move to the music of the questions that are alive in your life. Today's dare corresponds to the "Question Collection" tool from the Lifeseeds Toolkit.

Lifeseed #73—See Yourself as a Cycle of Change

73

Ever focused out there, we were fixed on a fractal of time, missing the multidimensional opportunity found right here, right now, within the portal that we are. We have been waiting to find some direction, forgetting it is we who are the eternal cycles of change.

FOCUS TEXT
Unlimited Direction

To this point in human history, our ideas of change have been defined by all that we have encountered along our journey through this life. What we see has been informed by the vision seen in our mind's eye.

We focus forward on the future and reach toward it. This is a good start we have made, but it is only a partial revelation. This is but one fractal of time — a singular direction limited by where we believe we have come from, by where we find ourselves right now and by where we have imagined ourselves to be going.

In truth, there is no need for reaching, for revelation is the very substrate from which patterns of change emerge. Likewise, change itself morphs and becomes multidimensional, no more limited by the shape and form of who we have been to ourselves and to others.

See yourself as a cycle of change, a work of art splashed with the life of color and the dance of the brush across canvas. You are the masterpiece and the master, the medium and the moment in which a creation is being born.

Direction becomes irrelevant. Commit to the dance, to everything, and to no thing at all. You have no need for remembering the words or mastering a tune, for you are the song itself and a melody rising in the wind, ever being formed and finding your resting place in the place the song was born.

LIFESEED
See Yourself as a Cycle of Change

Change frightens most of us. It unsettles us. We don't know what to expect. When it starts to happen in us and around us, our minds flash back to other changes that have unfolded.

The opposite is also true, for there are those changes we desperately desire. We believe that when this change or that change finally appears, *then* things will be alright and we can move toward our future. Both looking ahead to changes that will occur in the future when some circumstance changes *and* hinging ability to respond to change unfolding now on past experience represent two singular perspectives based on your life's experience in linear time.

The interesting thing about change is that as we gather up our internal energy and bring our full awareness to the moment of now, we begin to realize that we ourselves create change and affect our inner and outer environment, and therefore our experience of that environment in every moment. There is a ripple effect, and we are powerful creators and contributors to change.

The possibilities for your life are indeed infinite. You need only begin by being present and allowing the dance of your life to unfold.

DAILY DARE
Continuum of Possibility

Think about a desired change you wish to see in your life or in your environment. On a line with three dots, write a short phrase to note what is happening now, what you have been wanting to happen, and what represents the outcome you most desire. Then consider the many other possibilities and make a list of the most desirable outcomes in your Lifeseeds Journal. Be creative. Consider every situation that might bring about the change you desire. Realize the directions in which that change might occur are truly unlimited. Now remember you are the center of an ever-expanding sphere of infinite possibility, and there are things you have yet to imagine. As a body in motion and a cycle of change, you are free. Today's dare corresponds to the "The Shape of Possibility" tool from the Lifeseeds Toolkit.

Lifeseed #74—Engage in Value Redefinition

74

We saw so much as lost and wasted and longed to save ourselves. We seemed strangers to ourselves. Everything seemed an emergency. Desperately we searched for one another, forgetting again that the whole of our lives was a dance in a dream we chose.

FOCUS TEXT
Search and Rescue

So, ask not if you are enough. Ask not what more you must know in this moment. Know what you know. Allow yourselves to be revealed and then revel in the knowing and the being known, the sacredness of both the dawn of understanding and the shadow lands.

Redefine value. Engage in value redefinition. Find a way forward, yes. But also your way back. And into the layers of soul that blossom into possibility for ways forward you have not yet imagined. Trust the ripples of love to become waves that cannot drain you of you anymore than the ocean can lose its life by kissing golden shores.

Knowing you've no need for replenishment, see also that nothing is lost or wasted. You long for restoration, for salvation, for all to be set aright. In the mirror, you see a stranger — a life turned topsy-turvy, trunks of treasure sunken.

No one is lost to herself. You are not in need of saving.

This is mere illusion, the inverse of hope, a mirage of shipwrecked dreams. Flip the image and you have a voyage of extraordinary wealth and cause for celebration at the discovery that life is a dance within a dream we chose.

So, call off your search for one another. See at last the beauty of your being where you are and the gift of where you have perceived yourself to be. Fall into being, born anew to the miracle of a kaleidoscope of change. Soar beyond your sights of heaven and ground yourselves in the very being of who you are, indivisible.

Make way for generations of possibility waiting for emergence — here already when you abandon the shortsightedness of emergency.

LIFESEED
Engage in Value Redefinition

What if we were okay, just as we are, just as things are right now? What if everything was possible when we chose to see value and significance in ourselves and in the experience in which we find ourselves, no matter how lost we might feel within it? Maybe we have learned to attach meaning and value only to the sunny side of life and that elusive blue-sky day and disregard other things. Perhaps we assign meaning obsessively. Or maybe we believe everything, including ourselves and the light we bear, means nothing.

Stand in the center of your life connected to all that is most true and turn, turn, turn. See it all with fresh eyes. Choose a whole new way of being in relationship to what is now in you.

As you find value in all of it and connect the streams in your soul to these currents of life around you, remember that you will not lose yourself. This is a false belief many of us formed when we felt depleted by opening up. This feeling that we were losing ourselves came only because we had made the decision that we either needed something outside ourselves to be complete or we felt it was our responsibility to save another.

Our intentions were mostly honorable. We wanted wholeness. We just forgot where to look. We just didn't know we truly had a treasure and in fact were that treasure. We have distracted ourselves with all the fixing, saving, and wanting, failing to rest in the revelation always at work as we make our latest revolution around the sun.

DAILY DARE
Valuing the Patterns Being Revealed

What is the beauty of being where you are? How can you see life as a "kaleidoscope of change" revealing patterns of beauty? What would it look like in your life to give up the need to put all the pieces together again and simply be with the beauty of it all? Write about what you found to value here and now in your Lifeseeds Journal. Today's dare corresponds to the "Through the Looking Glass" tool from the Lifeseeds Toolkit.

Lifeseed #75—Stand in Sacred Time

75

We saw time stand still and understood it not. Still, we worried about running out of time; and, at the same time, we delayed our full expression in time. Ever waiting or in a hurry, we missed the promise wrapped up in our present.

FOCUS TEXT
Time Passages

There is the time you have known by the ticking of a clock, and there is another experience of time that is much different. You speak of time standing still. This is sacred time, a moment infused with the promise and fulfillment of a lifetime.

The truth is you have all the time you need. Not only is there no need for hurry; there is also no need to wait. The time is always now, and there is always time. And that time appears to meet your need. It also slips by if you choose not to live fully into it. Redeem your ticket to ride, and take all the time you need.

LIFESEED
Stand in Sacred Time

How do you see time? Is it on your side or has it become the enemy? Are you constantly adjusting, feeling as if you must hurry to catch up with life? Or perhaps you feel caught up in time, waiting on life to find and save you.

When we let time pass without redeeming it and living fully through it, we contribute to what may become a stockpile of regrets. How can you stand in the moment, in this day, and honor the time that is given by living into it? Through this particular passage of your life's journey, how can you be all of who you know yourself to be and move through with a confident grace, not in a hurry, not at a standstill waiting for time.

Meet time. Bring your whole heart to the day and watch with wonder as the hours expand your joy and move you across the river and into the promise of a life that is waiting even now for you.

DAILY DARE
Unprecedented Access

What does it feel like to consider that you have access to all the time you need? If you were a person who trusted time, what would that look like? How would your experience of life change if you were that person today? In your Lifeseeds Journal, assume that you are that person and capture a vision for how your day will unfold as you stand in sacred time. Today's dare corresponds to the "Sacred Time Traveling" tool from the Lifeseeds Toolkit.

Lifeseed #76—Breathe in Promise Revealed

76

We held our breath, but nothing seemed to happen. Still accustomed to looking in every direction but within, we saw so much but missed the point of the parallels and repeating patterns. We were on the verge of a radical discovery, awaiting a revelation that could only be revealed when we partook of it.

FOCUS TEXT
Parallels in Space and Time

Imagine the ancient pyramid, a golden home for souls transitioning, safe passage made more comfortable by reminders of a ruler's riches and reward.

Now, shift and see yourself, here and now, awakening to the all that is. You are a cup filled from center point of stillness that provides an abundant opening to the inner life facilitated by whispers of our remembered home beyond.

A tear in the fabric of your star-crossed universe or a gaping wound inside the human heart: they are one and the same. Mirror images are two halves of a whole, yet whole within the halves. This pattern replicates. Light is never diminished within the particles transformed as they transform the world they inhabit.

Into infinite darkness, light speeds its love. Love rushes in to spark a flame, revealing colors of life reflected in the glow of all that is. Embrace it. Release it. Breathe the promise revealed in the rise and fall of your body, caressed by every breath.

LIFESEED
Breathe in Promise Revealed

We have been accustomed to fearing death and transitions, and deep down if we are honest with ourselves many of us have little faith in our own ability to navigate life's rough waters. So when it becomes obvious the whole world is in state of transformation, intuitively we know we ourselves are simultaneously undergoing profound and significant change.

At such times, we are naturally attuned to the sweeping changes at play, on guard for what will unfold in our own lives. It is natural to wonder how we will be changed by the journey ahead. But to become entrenched in these wonderings and allow them to steal our breath denies us the life that is the gift of now. In such times, we can hold fast to all the ways we have been blessed in all that has unfolded already. Slowly and surely, the truth that we are stronger than we know is revealed.

Today, we are reminded to return to breath and to trust in our safe passage through space and time. In the stillness of the breath in to receive a life more abundant and in the breath out as we release all that is no longer needed we are filled to capacity with the assurance that all is well.

DAILY DARE
Transition Planning

Today we will plan for transitions. What change or transition lies ahead for you? What are your questions or uncertainties about how it will all unfold? Breathe in the promise of a life more abundant. Breathe out all that would keep you from it. Return to this page in your Lifeseeds Journal to record what you learn about yourself as you move through this life passage. Today's dare corresponds to the "Transition Planning Pyramid" tool from the Lifeseeds Toolkit.

Lifeseed #77—See the Intricate Beauty of Life Unfolding

77

We always looked out there, beyond, to heaven or a distant home. Forgetting this gift we gave ourselves, we were waiting for the gift of eternity which we thought could only come to us in the future. We are yearning to become free at last, unaware of the sheer veil that clouds the vision of glory we so diligently sought.

FOCUS TEXT
Unveiled

On Earth, so many of you who have had a glimpse of the hereafter choose to see it as separate from and other than. And then there are those of you who are more awakened, and yet, you, too, would cast aside the world that is your home in favor of the home you left behind.

This world is a world waiting to be born, held within the very womb of heaven's grace. You must be born to it first and allow its divine splendor to be revealed in due time. You come to Earth and are immersed in the slower yearning to become. Some of you grow impatient, for the veil between the truth within your hearts and its very beating is thin. You are blessed, and yet you remain blinded to the beauty of being where you are.

There are days you live in the here and now as if walking through a fog of forgetfulness. You have forgotten what you know: that on this journey, you yourself are the gift and the giver. You yourself gave up everything you knew to receive it all again. And here you resist receiving the very gift you asked for. Wake up! When you catch a single ray of truth, allow it to pierce that veil of separateness you have pulled between you here and you there. It is merely something you have used to fool yourself, to shield your soul from a truth you think might kill you. In fact, it will bring you back to the full and abundant life waiting for you where you are right now.

We are never really alone. We are connected in a matrix of soul, uniquely formed with intricate diversity and woven into whole worlds of universal love. It is the kaleidoscope of life, patterns being rearranged to the delight of the one gazing through the looking glass and diving in to where we have always belonged.

LIFESEED
See the Intricate Beauty of Life Unfolding

How many of us grew up singing about when we all get to heaven, about one day when it will all be alright? That sense of there and then being better than here and now is deeply ingrained in many of us. We are all looking ahead to life after life or looking back to what we think we had. Ours is a world of beauty, and each of us has a front-row seat uniquely positioned to experience the wonder as it unfolds.

The idea that we must awaken to see and know that beauty is also new to many, and it can seem more complicated than it actually is. It is a fine fabric of separation we ourselves have dropped, likely because at one time or another we were so astonished by the beauty we did not know what to make of it. After all, here we were still on Earth, in these funny bodies, in less than ideal circumstances. How could it be possible that this unfolding moment was all we ever needed?

Do you know what you know? Do you see what I see?

DAILY DARE
The Kaleidoscope of Life

Today, create your own kaleidoscope of life by seeking moments of intricate beauty in the unfolding of this day. In your Lifeseeds Journal, write all that is unveiled in this day. Allow yourself to see how these simple moments create a pattern of change, reflecting the beauty we so often overlook in the hurry of our lives. Today's dare corresponds to the "Patterns of Change" tool from the Lifeseeds Toolkit.

Lifeseed #78—Know that Beauty Begins Within

78

Having long ignored what lay inside, we forgot that beauty begins within. Appalled at all that was going wrong in the world, we gave little attention to our inner environment, forfeiting along with our responsibility for its condition, the abundant gifts waiting for us there.

FOCUS TEXT
Interior Design

Decorate your inner life with crisp thinking and the most luxurious of thoughts and emotions. Just as you would make your bed with the best quality sheets you can afford, spare no expense and handpick only the best thoughts and feelings — those that result in you being loved lavishly by you for the legacy you are. Begin always with the love you give to you.

Brighten up your inner space. Shed a little light. Clean out the dusty corners. While you're at it, set the mood, will you? Get a little ambience. Spruce up your soul, because whether you know it or not, you've got company. Guess who's coming for dinner? And lunch and breakfast, too?

You are!

So fill your heart with delicious experience. Absorb truth from the best books and ideas. Invite the prophets of old and modern-day pioneers to join you. Set your table in the wilderness.

Remember, for appetizers and salad, start on the outside and work your way in. For life's main course, work your way from the inside out.

LIFESEED
Know that Beauty Begins Within

What sort of home have you created within? Have you ever thought about hand-picking only the best thoughts? Do you intentionally clean out the clutter and sweep away old, dusty emotions to allow your inner light to flood your soul space?

Some of us have so long neglected the beautiful home these bodies provide that we hardly remember what inner exquisite comfort they provide. The wonder of this sanctuary within is astounding. Here, we are afforded complete sovereignty.

We may decide who may enter into this space. We can choose what thoughts and emotions we allow to linger here. When we are attuned to the desires of our hearts, we can create a space for those dreams and desires to be nourished and nurtured.

When we begin within, all manner of things become possible. It is as we connect to our core and design our interior space that we cultivate these feelings and experiences that will attract to us more of what we most desire.

DAILY DARE
Space Planning

Today, invest a few moment on an interior design project for your soul. What sort of environment do you intend to create? What will you bring into this space? What do you want to experience here? When will you visit? What sort of inner environment will set your soul free? Explore through journaling and doodling or art in your Lifeseeds Journal. Today's dare corresponds to the "Interior Design Plan" tool from the Lifeseeds Toolkit.

Lifeseed #79—Find What Feels Good

79

We compared ourselves to an imagined ideal, hiding from humble beginnings or a state of being we judged by the standards so long put upon us. Much time had passed since we stopped to consider our true heart's desires. We denied ourselves, sometimes putting the life abundant, there for us, on hold until we felt we could look some imagined part.

FOCUS TEXT
Adornment

Wear the colors of where you are and how your life unfolds. Do not be ashamed of a tattered beginning, of jeans frayed by your ventures into unexplored territory. These will shield you from the cold wind in the same way as do another's silk scarves and fine linen.

Refuse to accept that you are not meant to shop in the upscale boutique if that's what you want. And, really, if you like sitting around in your pajamas all day, then stop apologizing for it. No one's going to shoot you for it. Holy underwear is no less blessed.

Find what feels good. Never deny yourself as there is nothing worth caring for more. But do it because you love the gift of wrinkled flesh and tired knees, not because you might fall down and want to measure up should another opt to help you up. Worn shoes will take you where you need to go.

LIFESEED
Find What Feels Good

How often have we judged our worth or sized up another person based on exteriors — how they were dressed, what part of town they lived in, their cultural or religious affiliation, or even what school they attended? Sometimes we find ourselves living a life that no longer seems to fit, yet we feel obligated to keep up the role. Maybe we are worried about leaving someone behind. Perhaps we think we can't have that life because we don't have what it takes.

What do you love? Consider that. Never mind what you think you ought to do or where you have been told you belong. When and where do you feel most alive, most authentic, and most at home? What are you doing? How are you dressed? Who are you with?

What if you allowed a little more of that into your days? What if you let it be okay to stretch toward a whole new way of freeing yourself to be one hundred percent you?

DAILY DARE
Paper Doll Day

What life would you like to picture yourself wearing? Give yourself a paper doll day. Laugh a little, but seriously imagine anything is possible for you and your life. What feels good and most "you"? Envision you being fully you and feeling great. Draw an image and write about this version of you in your Lifeseeds Journal. Carry this image with you throughout this day, and find ways to lean into it. Today's dare corresponds to the "Paper Doll" tool from the Lifeseeds Toolkit.

Lifeseed #80—Choose and Choose Again

80

We saw now how we had left so many dreams for our life behind and thought it was too late. We secretly wished for something other than what we had and where we were and sometimes even who we had become or were pretending still to be. Yet, we felt powerless to change any of it. We cast choice aside, forgetting it was our birthright.

FOCUS TEXT
Changing Clothes

Or you might decide to change your clothes. If you desire a different life or maybe just a different look, picture yourself wearing that life. Try it on for size. Imagine changing your outfit, starting with socks and underwear. Dress for the successful moment of receiving all you desire to experience.

In the world you live in now, it is customary to accept so much as fixed and unchangeable: your family, your name, your home — even your chosen path or profession. Choice is your birthright. If you long to plow the field, try on a pair of overalls for size. If you want to experience the explorer's grand adventures, pick up the binoculars and see.

This is more than dressing the part. Step fully into the role you choose and open yourself to experience with the belief that you may always and only become what you choose to become.

LIFESEED
Choose and Choose Again

What dreams did you leave behind? What passions did you follow as a child? What if all the choices were still on the table? What if it wasn't too late, as you might have imagined, for you to move in the direction of a life more suited to you?

Grandma Moses was one of the world's foremost folk artists. She started painting when she was well into her second half-century. Who's to say you can't try on a new life for size? Start with what you knew you loved once upon a time.

Explore. Learn. Read. Dream. Discover. Allow that lost passion the space to breathe again in your life. Today, choose you. Imagine everything is possible, just for today. Then, choose it again tomorrow, if you'd like.

DAILY DARE
Lost Passions Treasure Map

Consider lost passions today. Begin by making a sort of treasure map of the things you loved to explore once upon a time. Maybe there are things you set aside or felt forced to leave behind. Perhaps there is something you've always been interested in but never allowed yourself to try. Draw doodles on the page to represent each passion or treasure. Then for one or two of the treasures you have represented, record an action that would allow you to begin to explore it further in your Lifeseeds Journal. Today's dare corresponds to the "Lost Passions Treasure Map" tool from the Lifeseeds Toolkit.

Lifeseed #81—Find the Experience that Brings Out Your Best

81

We bound ourselves to a fixed circumference, keeping to a designated field of experience. We lived lives defined by limitation, consumed by a litany of why we could not venture into all that lay unexplored in our lives and in our hearts.

FOCUS TEXT
Leaving Limitation behind

To move forward and beyond the restricted life, you must cut loose the ropes with which you bind yourself. Refuse to limit yourself to the designated field to which others might confine you and which you yourself see as the boundary of your experience.

This does not mean you must leave a particular field of experience. If you are content to run the bases, run them well. If you long to play a different sport, find your team. Scope out the perfect location for your next big game. Gather the equipment you will need. Study those who have done it best, and embrace the love of the game.

If you don't feel called out onto the playing field, walk on. Find the experience that brings out the best in you. Love your life. Empty it of every thought that tells you why you can't.

LIFESEED
Find the Experience that Brings Out Your Best

What were you once told about your life and the limits you must accept? What conclusion did you make about the boundaries of your life's experience? Have you considered what really brings you fully alive? Or are you simply following a script somebody handed you once upon a time?

So many of us go through life doing all the "right" things and make ourselves miserable. We create and impose a system of rules upon ourselves that water down both our engagement of our lives and the beauty of the gifts we have to share. We invent a whole host of reasons why we can't do the thing we most want to do. We block our own full expression and fulfillment.

Create a container within that you fill only with encouragement and expanded possibilities for your life and for your life's work. Seek out new experiences. Learn about what lights you up. Once you know what it is, do more of it.

DAILY DARE
New Experience Chooser

Take time to set the stage for the exploration of new experiences today. Consider what you want to explore or experience. What have you never tried? What is the experience you would like to have? Identify one or two individuals who have had such an experience. You don't have to know these people personally. Write down their names in your Lifeseeds Journal.

Now, consider if there are any tools or equipment you need or any special preparation. Where could you learn more about this experience and immerse yourself in it even more? Consider books, online videos, and friends who might share their insights. Leave a space to record what you love about this experience and how it connects you with the life within you.

Today's dare corresponds to the "Choice Jar" tool from the Lifeseeds Toolkit.

Lifeseed #82—Cultivate Perspective and Balance

82

We busied ourselves with the business and busy-ness of life, thinking we must always be doing something, on the way to somewhere. We missed the delights of the days. We failed to notice the wonder unfolding now, losing our balance as we favored forward momentum over stillness and the savoring of the moment.

FOCUS TEXT
Snack Time

    Savor the delights of doing nothing and seeing everything come clear. Watch the bliss bubble up like laughter in the glass from which you drink your life. Feel the warmth of the ale and the wide-awake feeling of the snowflake that settles on your cheek like a fresh kiss.

    Listen to the songbirds and the coyote's howl. Hear the distinct growl of traffic. Feel the turning of the day to night.

    Whatever course you choose for your life, give yourself times to dawdle. Go fishing. Stand in the stream and see how far you've come. Catch the fish and let him go. Look down river at the stones settled here. See the water pooling then finding once again its way in the direction of its home, moving from source to source, rising up and falling down, becoming again and again.

LIFESEED

Cultivate Perspective and Balance

Down time and lighter moments re-energize us, providing fresh fuel for exploring the edges of our lives. Do you allow yourself to just be? If we achieve and broaden our base of experience yet don't allow a space for truly *feeling* the joy and wonder of these experiences, what's the point, really?

Open your senses and appreciate the fullness of your life. Access your inner awareness to tap a whole new vision of who you are and are becoming. Free yourself from a fixed schedule that eliminates time to dream and a space to simply be.

We need those times of looking back and looking ahead while we stand in the stream and feel life's flow in us, through us, and around us. Take a break from all the doing, the moving forward, and the continual self-improvement. Momentum is only meaningful when it is balanced by time for stillness, relaxation, and evaluation.

DAILY DARE

Go Fish

It's time to put up the "Gone Fishing" sign. In other words, take a break today. Consider your daily or weekly schedule. Is there a specific time of the day or a block of time each week you could designate as "do nothing" time? Make a note in your Lifeseeds Journal and add this to your calendar now. Commit to being present to you without the need to accomplish anything at all. Today's dare corresponds to the "Do Nothing Dawdle" tool from the Lifeseeds Toolkit.

Lifeseed #83—Consider Form and Function

83

We feared death and life's daring that required changing form. We felt reduced or somehow diminished by such an experience, and so deprived ourselves of rich experience. All too often, we fixed ourselves to what seemed most safe and drew a circle for our lives based on this false center point.

FOCUS TEXT
Form and Function

You fear changing form, for you define yourself by the state of your being. You are so much more. You are not confined by the shape of your body nor restricted by its covering. You are not reduced to the accessorized life. Neither are you made invisible simply because you shift into spirit.

And when you fall softly to the ground and flow again into liquid possibility or rise in a vapor, the flow in which you find yourself is not mere necessity of transportation from one place to the next. Form can follow function. Or form can simply be form. It is by no means the total definition of who you are.

What is most important to you at a point in time may lead to a choice about the form you choose to take. Again, the function you choose to fill or follow is not meant to be the final word on the mystery of who you are.

Find your way through form and function and fly unencumbered by thoughts that tether you to a fixed circumference or bind you to a field extending from false center point.

LIFESEED
Consider Form and Function

How often have you told yourself something was simply not possible because of the shape you were in or how you looked? Do you believe that when you reach a certain age or your body becomes tired your life is essentially over? This is only one aspect of what it means to be human.

We are not our bodies. Our bodies often enhance our capacity to conveniently move from place to place or fulfill a specific function; however, our value and significance cannot be reduced to the shape we're in or our age.

In a similar way, when we choose to fulfill a specific purpose or take an action, we are not locking ourselves into a path forevermore. We have learned to limit ourselves because we have believed we had to stay within rigid expectations, whether we imposed those upon ourselves or they were handed down to us through the generations.

DAILY DARE
Draw a Bigger Circle

How big is the circle you have drawn for your life? How far do you allow yourself to reach? List all the things you believe you cannot do and the reasons why you believe you cannot do them. What if you began with a centering through aligned to your true nature?

Draw a bigger circle. Better yet, know there is no edge, no limit, no boundary to your being. Notice the thoughts that arise that would fix you to a false circumference. Explore this further in your Lifeseeds Journal. Today's daily dare corresponds to the "Line of Thought" tool from the Lifeseeds Toolkit.

Lifeseed #84—Embrace Change

84

Clinging to the familiar, we dared not leave the world we knew. We stuck to the same choices, a menu fixed and unchanging. We had lost altogether the adventure of our lives, afraid to dare explore what was unknown. This seemed to us reckless, as if we might put at risk or forfeit all that mattered most.

FOCUS TEXT
Become a Connoisseur of Change

Taste time. Sip it like fine wine. Raise your glass and toast this life. Drink it up, and then move on to another day and another tasting. Savor the moments — especially those that don't go as you had planned.

Try something new on the menu when you have the opportunity. When life serves up the same old same old, give thanks. And look for opportunities on today's ever-changing menu. Say yes to a new variety of experience that can open you up to the flow of good.

Take the long way home. Have breakfast for supper. Eat dessert first. Set off on an adventure without a full itinerary. Look for someone new to meet today, and learn something you never knew about yourself.

Change it up, and watch what happens next.

LIFESEED
Embrace Change

Hmmm. Savor the moments that don't go as planned. I don't know about you, but this is a new approach for me. It's far more natural to rush into an even greater success or to spiral down into that "I suck at life" place than to savor and remain present when things fall apart.

We're also creatures of habit who tend to find something that works or at least allow us to fly under the radar unnoticed. We find ways to "get by," and stick to that. We just want to keep things steady.

When is the last time you sought out a brand new experience? Change your routine. Dare to do it differently. Embrace all of you, no matter what and welcome change as the friend it wants to be to you.

DAILY DARE
New Choices

Think about the various areas of your life: Relationships. Meaningful work. Health. Financial flow and a state of abundance in all ways. What is your typical way of engaging with this area? Do you give yourself the option of trying a new approach? In your Lifeseeds Journal, list three new choices you'll make in each of the four areas above.

Notice what happens in the coming weeks and months. Remain unattached for what specifically appears. Open up to trying new ways and embracing new ideas about your life. Continue to embrace the new choices you have identified in each area. Learn to savor all the experiences of your life. Today's dare corresponds to the "Choose Again Life Transformation" tool from the Lifeseeds Toolkit.

Lifeseed #85—Celebrate Choice and Creative Contribution

85

We forfeited so many opportunities, the chance to choose again. Overwhelmed by choice at times and feeling we had no choice in the moment that followed, we forgot choice was an invitation to creative contribution. We thought we could make a mistake from which there would be no recovery. We tied love and grace to condition and so reduced our own experience.

FOCUS TEXT
Never Miss an Opportunity to Choose

Choice is a sacred gift. See all your choices like candy lined up before you, every piece of it delicious. Let your mouth water at the options and then go ahead; pick your favorite.

Go with what you know you love or pick the one that is calling out, "Choose me! Choose me!" And if you have no clear favorite, close your eyes and point your fingers and say yes to what it is that says yes to you.

Even if the decision that is before you seems serious and a painful choice between two lesser ways, see the very opportunity to choose as a gift of grace. Here you meet again the chance to express your creative being and contribute to the unfolding of life and all that is.

You are loved no matter what consequence follows your choice. You are treasured regardless of the result you co-create. You are cherished in the choosing, bathed in the blessed assurance of having received gift of choice.

LIFESEED
Celebrate Choice and Creative Contribution

Choice can drive us crazy. We may find we are overwhelmed by the sheer number of choices in our lives. We may feel we have no choice at all in the matter of our lives. Sometimes we find ourselves in situations where it seems all opportunity to choose a course has been taken from us. Yet, we may always choose how we respond and what gifts of ourselves we share.

How often do you consider what is saying yes to you? What is calling to your heart? When's the last time you checked in there?

At any point in our lives, we may choose to celebrate the choices we can make. In the words of the Serenity Prayer, we can choose to accept what we truly cannot change and change what we can. We can be intentional about who we are in any given situation.

What would you like to create in your life? How would you choose to respond to life's generous gift of choice?

DAILY DARE
Choose Wisely

Today, see how your point of choice is, in fact, your point of personal power. Think of a situation where you feel stuck, as if you have no choice. How would you choose to respond to this situation? Where will this potential choice lead you? What smaller, related choices are also yours to make? Explore these questions in your Lifeseeds Journal. Choose wisely. Today's dare corresponds to the "Choice Trail" tool from the Lifeseeds Toolkit.

Lifeseed #86—Hold Fast to the Truth of Who You Are

86

Wavering, we wondered if we had only imagined this new freedom that was ours. We listened again to others who told us we were merely dreaming and shortchanged the wildness and the wonder in the reduction of a truth that was essential. Coaxed back into an alluring half-wakened state, we stalled so near the finish line which was our beginning again.

FOCUS TEXT
Stand Your Ground

You feel as if you are waking from a long midsummer night's dream, but just as quickly you decide the new spiritual reality coming into focus is, in fact, the dream. When others insist that you are only dreaming of a more fanciful version of the facts, you relinquish your tentative hold on a truth you have barely begun to recover. When they say you have been mistaken in believing that you and they are great spirits unbound by time, you succumb and are coaxed back into the alluring half-wakened state that many of you reading are actually in.

When you are told that you are losing your grip on reality, stand your ground. When someone says your head is in the clouds, remind yourself that your heart finds its beat from the rhythm in the river of life. Smile at your friend and be grateful for the gift of imagination and for your spirit free and unencumbered by what you once saw as present reality.

Live the dream, and hold fast to the truth of who you are.

LIFESEED
Hold Fast to the Truth of Who You Are

We get glimpses, every now and then, tiny flashes that raise the possibility that life wants to give us more than we thought at first. If we do not dismiss this ourselves, others are all too willing to step into that role for us. We must stand our ground by remaining connected to what our hearts know as true. It is vital to our full experience of the love and joy life wants us to have.

It's about casting a vote in yourself for yourself and giving your heart the time and space it needs to be sure what it believes *before* you give others the opportunity to weigh in on the matter. In fact, we are better off when we listen to our lives. Bear witness to life as it unfolds around you and in you without inviting a cadre of opinions from others, which often serve only to confuse you.

Place your whole heart firmly in the ground of your being. Trust yourself to know what you know and open to all life would bring you. It is only when you stand your ground that your soul can take flight and soar free as it is meant to soar.

DAILY DARE
To Tell the Truth

Become a truth teller today. In your Lifeseeds Journal, complete these sentences:
If I told myself the truth, I would know that...
When someone else tells me I..., I will smile...
I will remind myself of the truth that I...
My dream of... is true for me.
Today, I trust that and bring my loving attention to my dream.
Today's dare corresponds to the "To Tell the Truth" tool from the Lifeseeds Toolkit.

Lifeseed #87—Unbind Yourself and Fly Free

87

Afraid again to trust ourselves and this life

far more expansive than once we had imagined, we climbed back

into the box. Bound by tradition, culture, and religion, we feared

what we might discover in realms beyond we now sensed we

were free to explore. We forgot we were created

free and beyond the bounds of fear.

FOCUS TEXT
Free Spirit

The big idea is this: you are bound only by your reluctance to allow your heart to beat strong with the life you are. You are restricted only when you fail to realign your growth in the natural direction of the source of your very breath. Unbind yourselves from all that would confine the reign of your great spirit to a set of rules or a border someone else would draw for you.

You are free to sample. You are free to choose.

Yet, when you climb back into the same small box again and again because you have been told that that is where you belong or because you were born into one tradition or another and have been told you must live in a certain way, eventually you come to believe that the box is the world.

Or worse, you become consumed by a crippling fear that the great unknown beyond the constricting confines of that beautiful box are the badlands, filled with danger. You begin to believe that, should you venture outside of your designated air space, you will be shot down and fall into forgetfulness. You begin to believe that the air inside the perimeter of the box is the source of your life, your sustenance — all that keeps you alive.

But a box — even an ornate treasure box — no matter how beautiful is, in the end, a box. If you love one present you have opened here, if it brings you comfort and joy and becomes a special place for you to be fully you then, by all means, return again and again. Just don't forget that the world is round, not square. It is a tiny blue dot unfolding with infinite choice and brimming with beautiful treasure boxes of every variety.

Above all else, know that you are created free, apart from fear, sealed in a timeless love unbroken by the human condition. Some have called it a love that will not let you go. Even if you have let it go and fixed yourself to a particular expression of that love, you are held safe and protected. The darkness that you imagine beyond can never extinguish your bright light.

LIFESEED
Unbind Yourself and Fly Free

Could it really be that simple — to allow our hearts to beat with their natural rhythms? Try this: fly like an eagle high above the place where you find yourself feeling restricted and held back from freedom. What can the eagle see that you cannot?

What are the boxes you have climbed into willingly in your life? What are the boxes you have felt forced to climb into? What are the ones you love and why have you come to love them so? These are the questions that can lead us to deeper truths about the ways we may have participated, sometimes unknowingly, in limiting our own freedom.

We set ourselves free when we change our perspective on freedom and safety. When we begin by trusting ourselves and trusting life, we naturally learn to fly, to explore, and to enjoy new experiences that present themselves.

Is your world a sphere expanding? Or have you boxed yourself in again?

DAILY DARE
Boxes, Packages, and Bows

Today, we'll take a look at boxes, packages, and bows. What are the boxes you have experienced in your life? Remember, not all the boxes are "bad" for you or undesirable. They are simply one experience of being and offer a single perspective or way of seeing ourselves and our lives.

What are the boxes you have avoided at all costs? Finally, what are the boxes you have felt forced to climb inside? It may be helpful to draw these boxes on a page in your Lifeseeds Journal and make some notes about your experience with each.

Notice their "packaging" — how they appear to you and how they are presented by others, who often do have your best interests at heart but who can never know the glory of your free spirit. Redecorate each box, thanking it for the ways it has brought learning and insight to your life. Today's dare corresponds to the "Box Decoration Project" tool from the Lifeseeds Toolkit.

Lifeseed #88—Risk the Journey

88

We wished to be great explorers. Ready for life's adventures, we stood confused, puzzled by the unfamiliar shores. We searched for a golden compass, forgetting our souls would always lead us home. We debated whether to risk life's journey full.

FOCUS TEXT
Intrepid Souls in Transit

You learn as children of the great explorers and wish you could explore new lands or sail upon the seas in search of all that is yet to be discovered. You can. You do! You are radiant and resplendent. And you are restless, ready for life's grand adventure.

You're off!

And still you stand on life's deck, looking around, confused. Are you waiting for permission to pull up the anchor and set sail? Puzzled by the unfamiliar bay in which you find yourselves, many of you choose to treat this life as if it were some shore leave.

Life is the adventure, my friends! Now is your voyage of discovery. Your very soul is the compass that will always lead you home. And if ever you feel uncertain, let the light of the stars lead you on. The story of your adventure on the high seas of this world will live on. But first you have to risk the journey.

LIFESEED
Risk the Journey

You are the explorer of your life. Are you still standing on the shore simply watching the days drift by? Do you dare to sail the high seas? Choose to risk life's journey. Say, "Yes!" to this daring adventure of your life.

Know that you have an inner compass that will always guide you in the direction of home. No matter how alone you may feel, you are indeed loved beyond measure and celebrated for the wondrous gift you are. Let the stars remind you of this truth.

You are on your way to a life of full expression. The journey will change you. You will discover unimagined lands and dive deep into an ocean of experience. Are you ready? Set sail and risk your life's grand adventure. Begin today.

DAILY DARE
True North

We all have a "True North" that will indicate to us from within whether we are headed in a direction aligned with our natural rhythms and the call of our soul. Think about it. How do you know when things are going well? How are you feeling in those moments? What's happening in your body?

In your Lifeseeds Journal, make some notes about the signs and indicators that can help you discern whether you are on a path true to the whole of who you are. Today, take at least one bold step that recreates this feeling. Invest ten minutes, or longer if you can, in an in-visioning practice that connects you to this feeling.

Imagine yourself in a situation that feels free. See all the details, and use every sense. Consider how it looks, sounds, feels, tastes, smells. Stay with it for as long as you can, and notice the way your body, heart, and mind feel as you do. Each day, look for the things that match this feeling state. Today's dare corresponds to the "Moving the Needle" tool from the Lifeseeds Toolkit.

Lifeseed #89—Retain Your Sense of Play and Adventure

89

We tamed our own spirits, buckling beneath the weight of all those people and systems who told us it was time to get serious about this life. We noticed when we were overlooked, our acts of daring courage and honor seemed invisible to those for whom we had risked our lives. We saw provisions that seemed meager and the humble way of our life. We stood and wondered what to do.

FOCUS TEXT
Pirates!

Move through life with honor, but don't forfeit your sense of play just because someone else would judge you or label you a miscreant. Know who you are and hold life and love sacred. Awaken to the thrill of another day on the high seas of life. Enjoy the adventure.

There may be an occasion in which you have been the hero but are not recognized as such. Let it be what it is and move on. Swash buckle your way if you must, and refuse to abandon your principles. Or your style. Savvy? Live with gratitude for what provisions you share, and live the grand adventure of the pirate's life.

LIFESEED
Retain Your Sense of Play and Adventure

We grew up and thought we had to be serious, so we put aside the very notion of play and adventure. But every explorer worth his salt has a bit of the swashbuckling pirate inside. This does not mean you lose all responsibility and forfeit purpose. On the contrary, as you embrace a playful spirit, you enhance your experience all along the way.

Celebrate the moments of discovery and also those when you just don't know. Learn to laugh at yourself. Be the hero of your own life. Maintain a connection to those principles that are most true for you. Above all else, sail on, captain! Move through your life with your own unique substance and style.

DAILY DARE
Color Yourself Permission for Fun

Create a series of colored permission slips to add a little fun and spice to your life. Get some construction paper or colored post-it notes, and let the colors mean something. Write one playful possibility on each. For example, red might stand for adventure and trying something new. Blue could represent swimming in an ocean of experience you've never visited before. Green could be for treasure and imagining the greatest story you can live, and yellow might be a new way to bring a sense of play and adventure to a daily task.

When you have mastered one, replace it with a new playful permission slip. Try them all in the next month. Write a reminder in your Lifeseeds Journal. Today's dare corresponds to the "Permission Slips" tool from the Lifeseeds Toolkit.

Lifeseed #90—Know the End Is the Beginning Again

90

In ourselves or in another, we came to face the hardest choice of all. Goodbyes had always seemed the end. We thought goodbye was forever and our lives a fleeting opportunity destined to be temporary. And so it was we delayed our voyages of discovery, fearing their eventual end, not realizing we are ever beginning again.

FOCUS TEXT
Goodbyes

Choosing when to stay and when to go seems sometimes the hardest choice of all. But in your choice to say goodbye, know you greet the moment of beginning again, again.

When I have gone, you may well remember me. Or in sweet forgetfulness imagine someone other than who I was. You may re-experience the first kiss or savor the memory of our last dance. Meet me in a field. Dare the rapids with me in a dream.

Carry me, and I will carry you.

LIFESEED

Know the End Is the Beginning Again

Along the way, we are sure to encounter moments that will require some goodbye. To dare our life's adventure, we may need to leave people, places, and things behind. It may be necessary to break away from communities or groups or settings which have been important to us in the past. We may need to move physically to a new place in order to welcome our best life.

Learning to say goodbye is one of the most challenging experiences for many of us. We have learned to associate goodbyes with pain. Some of us avoid the goodbye at all costs. But there is a whole new way of moving on that allows us to part with dignity and honor for ourselves, for the other, and for all that has been shared along the way.

What seems to be the end is really a true beginning again. This is the miracle of our lives. Hello, and welcome to all that waits for you! This is your beginning again.

DAILY DARE

Revisiting Goodbye

Consider all the ways you can embrace a whole new way of freeing yourself by reframing any necessary goodbyes into new beginnings welcomed even as you thank the experience and people, whether you have perceived them to be blessings or challenges, which you are releasing in love. What new experiences are you embracing and what are you saying goodbye to in order to welcome more light, life, and love into your life?

Create a collage of thanksgiving and gratitude to bless that you are leaving behind and step into the new beginning again of this day. Whether you are saying hello or goodbye or both in this day, know you are coming wholly to your life and living in full expression. Write about the experience in your Lifeseeds Journal. Today's dare corresponds to the "Gratitude Collage" tool from the Lifeseeds Toolkit.

p.s.

The end is really

the beginning again.

Where will you go from here?

How will you be
the LIGHT
you are?

How will you be
the LIFE
you are?

How will you be
the LOVE
you are?

Your Journey from Here

I AM SO GRATEFUL FOR EACH ONE OF YOU and the LIGHT, LIFE, and LOVE you bring to the world simply by being who you are. I am happy to have connected with more of my light, life, and love through these seeds for life, and I trust that you have found something that has connected you further to your essential self, journey, and truth. It is my heartfelt wish for you that you come more and more fully to life and live in full expression, sharing the whole of who you are and who you have come to be.

We are always learning from one another, and I want to hear from you how the Lifeseeds core curriculum has connected for you. Do you feel more connected to you whole self and your soul self? Do you have a better sense of your essential self, journey, and truth? I am also interested in considering ways to enhance this material and connect it in unique ways to those it might support. Please reach out with any suggestions you may have.

INVITATION TO THE DANCE OF YOUR LIFE • I would like to invite you to consider your next right steps on your unfolding journey. How will you continue your reconnection practice daily? What feels like the next right step for you? If you have not already joined the "90 Days to Life" online experience with daily videos and the complete audio and video collections for core passages and daily seeds for life, I invite you to do so. You can begin anytime and receive lifetime access to all program libraries and resources.

As a special thanks for your purchase of this book, I would like to extend a special offer to join me and the many who have embarked up on this soul journey in the "90 Days to Life" online experience at a discounted rate. Just click to purchase the course at DawnRicherson.com/90-Days-to-Life and enter the coupon code SEEDS20 for your savings.

THANK YOU • Thank you for the honor of connecting with you as we walked along this journey together. Trust that life is, indeed, working in your favor, and watch your world open up with wonder and the way of miracles. I wish you every blessing today and always.

With deep gratitude and appreciation,

Sharing Lifeseeds

Licensing Options for Use with Individuals and Groups

While the materials in this book are protected by copyright and only for individual use, a license to use the Lifeseeds Core Curriculum in your practice or setting is available for use with individual clients and groups. Options might include use in your professional practice or in a workshop or retreat setting. Please visit the website for updates on licensing options and contact me through my website with any questions you may have.

The Lifeseeds curriculum is a good fit for social institutions and programs that reach population groups who often benefit greatly from reconnection with themselves and as a result become contributors to society. Examples might include the prison population, those in recovery programs and receiving services from treatment centers, individuals who have been diagnosed with life-threatening diseases or facing life-altering situations, and those transitioning into more healthful ways of relating to others after experiencing trauma or abuse.

If you are interested in sponsoring a pilot project in your practice or organization, please contact me through my website, DawnRicherson.com.

About the Author

Dawn Richerson is a relentlessly authentic soul explorer and journey guide. She is the creator of Lifeseeds, a core curriculum for living in full expression and the author of the *Cultivating Essence* book series and other books on spirituality and wholeness. Dawn offers soul journeys and experiences online and through her Soul of Ireland retreats. Learn more at her website, DawnRicherson.com.

More Books by Dawn Richerson

Cultivating Essence from the Matrix of Soul

Awakening the World Within

Finding Our Forward Flow

Embracing a New Vision

All Systems Go

Journey to the Heartland

Vist DawnRicherson.com/Books
to browse all books and audiobooks.

www.ingramcontent.com/pod-product-compliance
Lightning Source LLC
Chambersburg PA
CBHW060512300426
44112CB00017B/2632